I0039483

GRAPPLING WISDOM

GRAPPLING
WISDOM

JOSE M. FRAGUAS

EMPIRE Books

P.O. Box 491788, Los Angeles, CA 90049

Disclaimer
Please note that the author and publisher of this book are NOT RESPONSIBLE in any manner whatsoever for any injury that may result from practicing the techniques and/or following the instructions given within. Since the physical activities described herein may be too strenuous in nature for some readers to engage in safely, it is essential that a physician be consulted prior to training.

First published in 2006 by Empire Books.
Copyright © 2006 by Empire Books.

All rights reserved. No part of this publication may be reproduced or utilized in any form or by any means, electronic or mechanical, including photocopying, recording, or by any information storage and retrieval system, without prior written permission from Empire Books.

Empire Books
P.O. Box 491788
Los Angeles, CA 90049

First edition
05 04 03 02 01 00 99 98 97 1 3 5 7 9 10 8 6 4 2

Printed in the United States of America.

Library of Congress: 2006009384
ISBN-10: 1-933901-12-8
ISBN-13: 978-1-933901-12-1

Library of Congress Cataloging-in-Publication Data

Fraguas, Jose M.
  Grappling wisdom / by Jose M. Fraguas.
    p. cm.
  Includes index.
  ISBN 1-933901-12-8 (pbk. : alk. paper)
  1. Martial arts--Quotations, maxims, etc. I. Title.

GV1102.F73 2006
796.8--dc22

2006009384

"Everything should be made as simple as possible, but not simpler."

—Albert Einstien

DEDICATION

This book is dedicated to you—the practitioner of the grappling arts. Your discipline, passion, and dedication served as the inspiration I drew upon to create the best book I could.

ACKNOWLEDGMENTS

Many people were responsible for making this book possible, some more directly than others. I want to extend our gratitude to all those whom so generously contributed their time and experience to the preparation of this work. A special thanks to designer Patrick Gross. I also want to thank Bill Curry, as well as my family, whose discernment is always tempered with kindness.

A word of appreciation is also due to Marcus Boesch, Holly Stein, Tami Goldsmith and Hal Sharp for their generosity supplying of great photographic material. Without their support, this book would not exist.

You all have my enduring thanks.

—Jose M. Fraguas

About the Author

Born and raised in Madrid, Spain, Jose M. Fraguas began his martial arts studies with judo, in grade school, at the age of 9. From there, he moved to tae-kwondo and then to kenpo-karate, earning a black belt in both styles. During this same period, he also studied shito-ryu karate-do. He began his career as a writer at age 16 by serving as a regular contributor to martial arts magazines in Great Britain, France, Spain, Italy, Germany, Portugal, Holland and Australia. Having a black belt in three different styles allows him to better reflect the physical side of the martial arts in his writing: "Feeling before writing," Fraguas says.

In 1986, Fraguas founded his own book and magazine company in Europe, authoring dozens of books and distributing his magazines to 35 countries in three different languages. His reputation and credibility as a martial artist and publisher became well known to the top masters around the world. Considering himself a martial artist first and a writer and publisher second, Fraguas feels fortunate to have had the opportunity to interview many legendary martial arts teachers. He recognizes that much of the information given in the interviews helped him to discover new dimensions in the martial arts. "I was constantly absorbing knowledge from the great masters," he recalls. "I only trained with a few of them, but intellectually and spiritually all of them have made very important contributions to my growth as a complete martial artist."

Jose Fraguas started his training in Gracie jiu-jitsu in the late '80s with several members of the Gracie family and continued for over a decade. "The art was not as big as it is today," Fraguas recalls, "and there was a feeling of being on the cutting edge of something significant and important. Years later, when I met Helio Gracie for the first time, I realized that the easy-going attitude and high technical level his sons displayed was simply a direct reflection of his own expertise and personality."

"I would love to mention the members of the Gracie family who spent so many hours in private and group classes sharing the art with me," Fraguas laughs, "but I'm afraid that naming them as being responsibility for my grappling skills would make them feel more pain than pride. They know who they are, and they know how much I appreciate their patience."

Steeped in tradition yet looking to the future, Fraguas understands and appreciates martial arts history and philosophy and feels this rich heritage is a necessary steppingstone to personal growth and spiritual evolution. His desire to promote both ancient philosophy and modern thinking provided the motivation for writing this book. "If the motivation is just money, a book cannot be of good quality," Fraguas says. "If the book is written to just make people happy, it cannot be deep. I want to write books so I can learn as well as teach. Martial arts, like human life itself, are filled with experiences that seem quite ordinary at the time and assume a fable stature only with the passage of the years. I hope this work will be appreciated by future practitioners of the arts."

The author is currently living in Los Angeles, California, where can be contacted at: **mastersseries@yahoo.com.**

INTRODUCTION

As early as I can remember, my house was filled with books. Many of these books—some new, some old—were excellent collections of quotations. My father and mother clipped quotes from magazines or newspapers, and even wrote some themselves and posted them on kitchen cabinets, the refrigerator and other special places for the family to see.

There are many pleasures to be derived from a book on quotations. There is the relief of finding something that has been buzzing in our minds, there is also the pleasure of finding some thought of which we approve but which we have not managed to express clearly and there is a purely retrospective delight. Of course, wisdom is meaningless until our own experience has given it meaning.

Through my childhood, reading and rereading these quotes has helped me to replace negatives thoughts with strong and positive alternatives. While words are not substitutes for the difficult physical and mental training required to master the martial arts, they are a relevant aspect of the transmission and the learning process of every student. *Grappling Wisdom* is an anthology of the best words said by the great masters of the grappling arts. It examines different elements of the arts, including its tradition, philosophy, general training, sport competition, self-defense, et cetera.

All the masters have expressed similar ideas in very different ways. Regardless of the words they used, there must be truth in the philosophies and principles that so many different people have believed in and lived by—and in some cases—died for. The more I researched, the more I realized that those great masters are more like you and me than they are different. They had difficult days and seemingly impossible hurdles, yet they endured and prevailed.

I have made every effort to present each quotation within its context as accurately as possible. In philosophical matters, it is syntax—more than vocabulary—that needs to be corrected. Due to the limitations of language and linguistic expression when dealing with philosophical and spiritual matters, it is easy to understand why some of the ideas and principles of these masters are so complex, subtle and intricate—particularly if the ideas are studied out of context. If you try to apply some of these ideas to your own life, don't forget that it is easier to quote somebody else than it is to really understand what they meant by saying it. There are obvious dangers in using words without being sure what we really mean. But there is another less obvious danger in trying to provide exact definitions—the danger is that we may think we have succeeded. As the philosopher Bertrand Russell wrote: "There is no more reason why a person who uses a word correctly should be able to tell what it means than there is why a planet which is moving correctly should know Kepler's laws." I respectfully would like to advise the reader to *listen* not to the words of the masters but to *what* they really meant when they said those words. The way of the martial arts produces a practitioner torn between the art and the mystic. The way of the artist and the way of the mystic are similar, but the mystic lacks a craft ... the physical techniques. The craft (physical training) keeps the artist in touch with the remarkableness of the world and in relationship to it. Therefore, philosophy without hard physical training is useless.

This book originated more than 20 years ago as a personal manuscript of life-affirming quotations taken from legendary martial arts masters for my own personal use. As I had the great opportunity to keep interviewing many of the greatest grapplers in the world, the pages of the manuscript kept increasing until one day my mother asked me: "What are you planning to do with all these quotations?" As soon as I answered, "I don't know," she was pointing with her finger to the shelves of one of the bookcases at home where the complete collection of books on quotations was. She simply smiled and left the room.

Meeting the masters and having long conversations with them allowed me to do more than simply scratch the surface of the technical aspects of their respective styles. It also helped me to research and analyze the human beings behind the teachers.

Years before anyone ever heard of any of them, they devoted themselves to their arts, often in solitude, sometimes to the exclusion of other pursuits most of us take for granted. They worked themselves into extraordinary physical condition and stayed there. They ignored distractions and diversions and brought to their training a great deal of concentration. The best of them got as good as they could possibly get at performing and teaching their chosen art, and the rest of us watched them and, leading our balanced lives, wondered how good we might have gotten at something had we devoted ourselves to whatever we did as ferociously as these masters embraced their arts. In that respect, they bear our dreams.

Most of what passed as human wisdom is merely the post-examination gabble of excited individuals trying to guess how the new lessons will explain the old questions of life and martial arts training. Anything is fresh on the first hearing ... even though others may have heard it a thousand times through a score of generations.

In the spring of 2002, I finished the first draft of this work, took the manuscript and sent it to several grappling masters. It was exciting to hear their comments. Many of them wrote kind words that they wanted me to use to support the project. Unfortunately, some of them won't see the final printed work, because they shed their mortal skin and returned to the sacred battlefields where the true warriors fight their battles. Their words are in this book because without them this work would never be completed.

More than three decades after my mother pointed to that old bookcase, here is the final work. Books are an essential part of my life and they have opened new and exciting avenues of life. My goal is to share these thoughts with as many people as possible. I hope this collection provides comfort and inspiration for all martial artists—regardless of style—and for the casual browser and reader. If you, the reader, find this work useful as both a guide and a reference work and discover some unexpected sayings, the book will have served its purpose.

Enjoy.

—Jose M. Fraguas

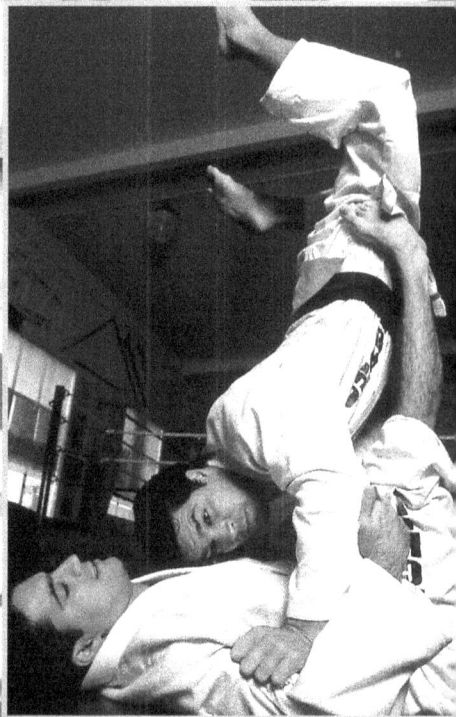

GRAPPLING
WISDOM

I started training seriously in martial arts when I moved out of my parents house. They never wanted me to train because they let me train taekwon-do when I was 14, and after two weeks I broke somebody's nose in a street fight.
Bas Rutten

I began my training in judo and my teacher taught the art in a very street-fighting oriented format. It was not sport judo but a self-defense approach. He really emphasized the street element.
Carlos "Caique" Elias

Jiu-jitsu training was a very natural thing at my home. Practicing jiu-jitsu was like eating, brushing my teeth, or sleeping. No more, no less—something natural and logical to be done on a daily basis.
Carlos Gracie Jr

I started training in 1974 in Minneapolis, Minnesota, when I was in 4th grade. I was diagnosed with ADD and my mother thought that it would be a good idea to get me involved in some kind of physical activity, so she signed me into judo classes.
Eric Paulson

A true budo man knows how to behave, he displays all the true qualities of a warrior, but as a warrior he knows how to fight and face death with no fear. Nice words should be spoken at the proper time, but the sword should be drawn when necessary.
Jon Bluming

Find the right kind of partner. Don't hurt yourself training with reckless people who don't care for technical refinement and are only interested in an uncontrolled grappling situation. These training partners won't help you improve. Be focused and train hard.
Fabio Santos

In some aspects I am a traditionalist, but I also believe in changing and adding things from other styles to you system.
Gene LeBell

I started martial arts when I was five years old. A sambo champion saw me and came to my house to take me to train.
Gokor Chivichyan

Ken and I used to train five hours a days for five days a week. We used to do a lot of different exercises and I got hooked. I remember I had to do 500 free squats, sit-ups, push-ups and leg lifts and then fight Ken for another half an hour!
Frank Shamrock

My older brother Carlos learned the art its Japanese version, from a Japanese immigrant named Esai Maeda, who taught him the art out of respect for my father, Gastao Gracie, who had helped him get established.
Helio Gracie

Carlos Gracie Jr. was our teacher from the beginning. When you say jiu-jitsu you have to link it to the Gracie family.
Jean Jacques Machado

I was hyperactive and I showed interest in martial arts, so my father took me to practice with one of my cousins, Vinicius Ruas, a judo instructor. I practiced only a few months then I switched to boxing.
Marco Ruas

You can sit back and claim that you're the best, and sit on your laurels. I guess it's a fear of failure, the reason people don't go out and try.
Mark Kerr

I had a very difficult time in the beginning. Nothing flowed. Nothing came easy. And this was a good thing as it taught me the value of out-working my opponents—of spending more time on the mat than they did. It taught me that to set goals and achieve them.
Matt Furey

I started in sambo when I was 10 years old. At that particular time the sambo training focused more on stand-up techniques—ground techniques were few in comparisons to all the throws and standing fighting techniques.
Oleg Taktarov

The Gracie challenge was created to put our system to the test and this is something very hard to keep up.
Relson Gracie

Almost every day that you train, you learn something new if you keep your mind open. If you're never out-learned, you'll never be out-fought.
Bas Rutten

My father loved judo and he used to train several times a week.
I wanted to do the same so I began going with him.
Renato Magno

I started competing at six years old, and since then I've been involved
in the sport aspect of jiu-jitsu, just training and competing.
Rickson Gracie

I love jiu-jitsu and I love to compete in jiu-jitsu so that is what I have
done. Professional fighting is a much different step. You have to love,
100 percent, the fighting game.
Rigan Machado

Jiu-jitsu is jiu-jitsu. What I mean by that is that if you have
a limited amount of time to train, then put as much time as you
can into developing your technique. Forget about anything else.
Jiu-jitsu should be your main goal.
Carlos "Caique" Elias

I was practically born on the mat.
I can't think of any period of my life
when I was not training or teaching
jiu-jitsu.
Rorion Gracie

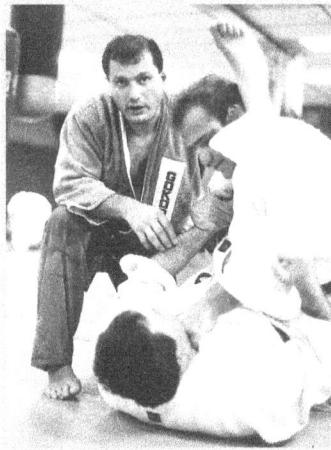

I started to train BJJ when I was 3. At the time I really didn't know what I was doing, I'd go to the academy to play soccer dressed in a gi.
Royler Gracie

Jiu-jitsu is an exceptional art. I respect all arts, but if you don't know jiu-jitsu, your art is not complete.
Wallid Ismael

Knowing how to massage was a requirement for second degree black belt. You needed to know how to heal the body, not just harm it.
Wally Jay

I trained in muay Thai for about two years. When I started training in jiu-jitsu, I kept training in muay Thai. A few months later, however, I gave up muay Thai.
Carlos Baretto

Competition classes and training for athletes who are going to compete should be addressed outside the normal classes. It is something specifically for those individual who spend a lot of time in jiu-jitsu.
Carlos Gracie Jr

I like jiu-jitsu the best, followed by wrestling and then boxing. I like judo the least because it has too many rules.
Vitor Belfort

Almost two decades after, and I haven't lost any interest since the first day I stepped on the mat.
Wander Braga

I was about eight years old at the time, and the doctor said I would never walk again because I had polio. Imagine you can't move your legs. It was pretty depressing.
Willy Cahill

Whenever the gym was open, you could go in there any hour of the day and you'd see people training. So you had to train hard because these guys were trying to take your position away on the team.
Rico Chiapparelli

The style is only as good as the individual. If the kickboxer is better than the grappler, the kickboxer will win. If the grappler is better, he will prevail. It's that simple. In MMA events, it is about the athlete because the technical structure is pretty similar.
Fabio Santos

In teaching I found a new venue. I always loved to teach but being a fighter leaves almost no time to share your knowledge with others. You have to be selfish and think about yourself at all times.
Eric Paulson

Wrestling has been there for many years, but nobody ever looked at it as a fighting art until wrestlers started to compete in the UFC and win.
Randy Couture

I was a big kid, and I wanted to start training in something. In the section of Rio where I lived, I saw some guys training in what turned out to be luta-livre, so I checked it out.
Hugo Duarte

Wrestling is a different form of grappling that can create some problems for a BJJ practitioner due to its ways of attacking, defending and controlling an opponent on the ground.
Paulo Gillobel

My father Carlos was the first great fighter of the Gracie family. In addition to jiu-jitsu, he enjoyed boxing and was the Brazilian boxing champion.
Carley Gracie

My style differs from other styles of Brazilian jiu-jitsu in the sense that I am always inventing and evolving new techniques and fighting strategies, refusing to let my jiu-jitsu become stagnant or outdated. If you're not going forward, you're going backward.
Carlson Gracie

When you are a professional fighter you need to find different ways to keep yourself motivated. In the beginning money and exposure may be the reason but after a while you need more than that.
Frank Shamrock

My jiu-jitsu training was always with my father, my brothers—Rickson and Rorion—and also with Rolls Gracie.
Royce Gracie

My original goal was simply to learn self-defense, nothing else. But I quickly fell in love with jiu-jitsu and just couldn't stop.
Fabio Gurgel

I was constantly called haole (outsider). In Hawaii, the testosterone level is high, and the people are very fast to fight. People will fight at the drop of the hat. If you don't stand up for yourself and fight, you'll get a reputation as a punk and will get picked on more.
John Lewis

I always tried to uphold the meaningful and ethical values that the previous masters have cultivated and developed.
Fabio Santos

I started jiu-jitsu because I was hyper as a kid in the Rio de Janeiro area. My mom wanted to put me in sports to calm me down.
Cleber Luciano

I studied with Carlson Gracie when I was 16 and already had a blue belt. Carlson's academy was a like boot camp! The eliminations inside the academy for the right to compete were harder than the actual tournaments themselves!
Rodrigo Medeiros

Technique is the first thing to develop, and if you have a limited amount of workout time then that should be your priority. Any additional time can be spent on supplementary training.
Gokor Chivichyan

It is important to get the basics from one instructor and develop a deep understanding of them. Later, if you have the opportunity to expand your training under other instructors, you may get some personal points to add to your previous knowledge.
Helio "Soneca" Moreira

To be an elite competitor at the Olympic level, you have to dedicate all your time to the sport you choose.
Jason Morris

You have to know how to take care of yourself on the islands. You can't grow up in Hawaii without getting into fights.
B.J. Penn

Besides Brazilian jiu-jitsu, I have also been training in boxing, karate and muay Thai. These are good fighting systems, and I think they complement jiu-jitsu very well.
Nino Schembri

I am basically—by nature—a fighter. I started when I was 10 years old and that continued as a teen-ager. I was forced to learn how to protect myself at a very young age so I was always down with defending myself.
Ken Shamrock

In modern jiu-jitsu competitions, fighters are using force and pure strength to compensate for the lack of polished technique. And that is not good.
Helio Gracie

Japan was my turning point for understanding the sacrifice required to become a world champion or compete at the Olympic level.
Mike Swain

I have always been attracted to jiu-jitsu, so I never felt the need to go to another martial art. I don't recommend that anyone jump from style to style to find the perfect style.
Leo Vieira

Everyone should have takedowns in his routine. Jiu-jitsu has takedowns, but people only focus on ground techniques.
Marcio Feitosa

Rolls was not only my teacher but also my friend ... a friend who influenced my life in many ways way beyond the jiu-jitsu. But life had to go on.
Fabio Santos

You can't have the mindset that training is merely something to do to kill time. Don't go to the academy and merely go through the motions. Have a goal in mind every time you train—and train regularly.
Renato Magno

Rolls Gracie was always searching. Not only did he beat everyone in jiu-jitsu, he used to go to judo tournaments and win everything. He was good in anything that he tried because [he was so] confident.
Carlos Valente

For my skin condition I wore gloves which made me a target for the other children to pick on. That resulted in many street fights which, by the way, I never lost.
Bas Rutten

I don't need to punch my opponent into pulp to feed my ego. It's a sport. I will do whatever it takes to win but no more. I don't need to hurt anyone to prove that I can win a fight.
Rickson Gracie

I started jiu-jitsu with Relson Gracie and also trained extensively with Rickson Gracie. They not only gave me an extensive amount of technical knowledge but also spent a lot of time educating me in the different aspects of jiu-jitsu. The training was tough.
Carlos "Caique" Elias

I didn't have a true appreciation of what the art was all about until I was around 14 or 15 years old. That's when I became more interested in technical development, competition, and in improving my game.
Carlos Gracie Jr

My brother was already wrestling so for me the idea of grappling with another guy wasn't strange at all. To be totally honest, judo was the last thing I wanted to do at that time. I enjoyed playing other sports like hockey, baseball and football but judo...no way.
Eric Paulson

I have a real passion for teaching. I really love to teach; it makes me feel happy. The process of sharing something with someone and making that person happy, it's a great experience for me. It's not about money. It's about personal satisfaction.
Frank Shamrock

The genuine teacher is there to help the student identify obstacles; discuss possible solutions. He shouldn't be comfortably perched upon some distant pedestal.
Rorion Gracie

Thanks to Rickson Gracie, I started to feel motivated again. I started to enjoy the training, and I finally regained the passion for what I was doing.
Fabio Santos

A lot of the finishing moves that I learned in catch wrestling are illegal in judo competition, but they are great for fighting and self-defense, so why not use them?
Gene LeBell

Be gracious at all times, be honest with yourself and chase your dreams because your time is limited.
Randy Couture

I watched the classes taught by my brother Carlos but I wasn't allowed to participate due to my physical condition. I used to sit there every single day, memorizing all the moves in my mind.
Helio Gracie

I think that everyone today that knows Brazilian jiu-jitsu learned it, directly or indirectly, from a member of the Gracie family. Everyone should be grateful to them for that.
Jean Jacques Machado

I started with sambo wrestling in 1968 in Armenia. A few years later I began to train in judo. It was natural after having a foundation in submission grappling. I didn't know what judo was, but it was very familiar with ground work and so I gave it a try.
Gokor Chivichyan

To be a master in capoeira, one must be an artist. You have to play musical instruments and sing songs as well as fight. But I only dedicated myself to fighting; I could not sing and did not learn the instruments. I guess my future was not in the music business!
Marco Ruas

If you're supposedly the best fighter in the world, you have to go out there and compete against the best to prove it. I just can't sit back and semi-retire and be happy with yourself. If you're considered the best, you have to prove it.
Mark Kerr

In February 1959, I arrived at the Kodokan and the feast started. In November 1959 the President of the Kodokan called me in his office and Draeger as translator told me that I was chosen to join the kenshusei in which there were the 25 best judoka from Japan all together in a special class. I was very honored and who was the head teacher? Mifune Sensei himself!
Jon Bluming

When I started training in Chinese martial arts, though, a shift took place. For some reason learning wrestling holds and such got a lot easier.
Matt Furey

Sambo has a lot of groundwork but even at the time, in competition, the fighters didn't go to the ground much. They preferred stay up and grapple on their feet.
Oleg Taktarov

Remember that there is no substitute for hard training, and it is not the quantity of time spent training but the quality.
Helio "Soneca" Moreira

Sometimes you have to adapt to the circumstances and roll with the punches. Adapting to your current life situation is something that a lot of people don't know how to do.
Fabio Santos

During more than 70 years the different members of the Gracie family have been trying to prove that the jiu-jitsu method developed by the Gracie's is a great and effective self-defense system.

Relson Gracie

After I began studying jiu-jitsu, the combination of the two arts was very interesting. I used judo for the stand-up aspects of throws and takedowns, but on the ground my technique was pure Brazilian jiu-jitsu.

Renato Magno

Jiu-jitsu offers a very special way for you to understand yourself. You can understand your limitations; you can improve your patience, sensitivity, coordination, and sportsmanship; you learn how to lose and how to win; and you learn how to be respectful.

Rickson Gracie

Hard work and dedication will pay off in judo, and more importantly, in life. Martial arts teach that lesson very well.

Jason Morris

A professional fight does not give me the same feelings that I get from Brazilian jiu-jitsu.
Rigan Machado

The most significant memories I have, are those of my father teaching. His ability to explain with passion and dedication was unique and entertaining.
Rorion Gracie

Brazil is the land of soccer and you generally give your kids a soccer ball, but I was given a gi. So my father and my brother Rolls, in order to get me and the other kids interested in coming to class and to the academy, made us play soccer dressed in a gi.
Royler Gracie

For a while I did the Gracie diet but mine is a little more radical. I keep a vegetarian diet.
Wallid Ismael

Life changes and you have to schedule your training sessions accordingly—especially if you are not a professional jiu-jitsu teacher.
Fabio Santos

You have to know how to change and adapt to different environments and circumstances. I've always disagreed with adhering to tradition just for tradition's sake.
Wally Jay

Don't do something just because you read it, saw it on a video, or somebody told you. Find out if it really works first. This is important for any person who wants to train in martial arts.
Bas Rutten

I love muay Thai, and I respect it. At the time I started jiu-jitsu, however, there was a great rivalry between the different martial arts in Rio—especially jiu-jitsu and muay Thai. So I had to choose one or the other.
Carlos Baretto

I always say that tomorrow is a promissory note, yesterday is a cancelled check and today is cash on hand. That is the way that we should all live our lives.
Vitor Belfort

I can't think of my life without thinking of jiu-jitsu. What I am today is a direct product of the philosophy and teachings of the art.
Wander Braga

I got some help from my father's judo instructor. He used to put herbs on my legs and give me a massage while I was confined to the bed. About a year later I was out of the hospital and free of polio.
Willy Cahill

The key is to balance every single element in your training so that one aspect will help the others. The secret is balance, not only in martial arts but in life as well.
Carlos "Caique" Elias

There are certain factors you can always control, and conditioning is one of them. You can always be in great condition.
Rico Chiapparelli

I truly have a lot of respect for MMA and especially the UFC. It revolutionized the martial arts world and brought realism to it.
Randy Couture

Although jiu-jitsu was not as big as it is today, it was still well-known because of Helio Gracie. It would have been easy for me to join with them, but they always had such an attitude towards all of the other martial arts that it turned me off.
Hugo Duarte

I truly think that wrestling complements Brazilian jiu-jitsu very well. You need to know how to make both arts blend in a smooth way.
Paulo Gillobel

I got my major in Physical Education from the University of Gama Filho in Rio de Janeiro. Then Rorion Gracie called me and invited me to teach at his school in Torrance, California.
Fabio Santos

Jiu-jitsu training is very similar to life itself. To receive the most out of your training you have to be capable of seeing these similarities.
Carlos Gracie Jr

I was born into a family of fighters. We were raised in an enormous house with 28 bedrooms, and there were always many brothers, cousins and students of the family around practicing their jiu-jitsu. I naturally learned how to approach a "fight" early.
Carley Gracie

I was always fighting against people who were bigger than I was, so naturally I would end up on the bottom. Fortunately, I could dish out a lot of punishment from there.
Carlson Gracie

For me, training jiu-jitsu was a normal thing in my life. I never felt pressure because my father understood that kids don't like to learn … they like to play.
Royce Gracie

Nobody likes harsh words, but the point is that everybody likes to talk.
Fabio Gurgel

When I came to L.A., I met a man (Dan Koji) who would change my life. He was from Japan and had his own system that I can best describe as muay Thai for the street. He called it shokondo.
John Lewis

The instructor's personal training has to be different than the teaching aspect because it's a different thing. Your training can't be your teaching in class.
Eric Paulson

The Brazilian jiu-jitsu practitioner must know how to wear his opponent down. When the opponent is worn out, he's unfocused and his concentration level is down. That is when we use our brain and intelligence because our opponent can't think clearly.
Fabio Santos

The advantage to having my own school is that I can teach the way I want ... on my own schedule. It is better. I have more freedom.
Cleber Luciano

I think the methodology you use to teach is important. You have to stress the basics and always keep going back to the basics. The simple things are hard to teach and hard to learn.
Rodrigo Medeiros

A man must do what he really wants to do. If you are not up to it whatever it is then don't do it because you will never be happy and it will never bring you the proper rewards.
Jon Bluming

In Brazil, it is simply jiu-jitsu and it comes from the Gracie family. But I know it is important to use the term "Brazilian" so people can differentiate the system the Gracie family created and the system developed from Japanese forms of jiu-jitsu.
Helio "Soneca" Moreira

When you are young and begin martial arts training, almost everything is absorbed immediately and stays with you for the rest of your life.
Jason Morris

I got my blue belt in six months and my purple belt in 18 months. Seven months later I got my brown belt. Eight months after that I got my black belt. So, it took me exactly three years and four months to get my black belt.
B.J. Penn

Jiu-jitsu is about using the proper strategy and tactics at the right time. You don't look for the technique. On the contrary, you set an environment in which the opponent gets himself in trouble.
Fabio Santos

If you want to be a real fighter and prove yourself in MMA then you are in for hard work and a very hard game.
Jon Bluming

Unfortunately, I have seen great jiu-jitsu fighters train in kickboxing for a few years and then go into a fight and forget all about jiu-jitsu and just punch and kick!
Nino Schembri

My background is submission wrestling where there are no positions and all the positions you may find yourself in are equally important. Neither one scores points. I don't enjoy the pure grappling events like Abu Dhabi because I would have to restructure my system to fit into that type of fight and, it isn't worth my time. I'm fighter and I fight, I don't go out there just to roll around with a guy.
Frank Shamrock

Walking into the ring knowing it was one-on-one with no weapons or foreign objects besides your opponent was actually a relief.
Ken Shamrock

I think a good solid boxing and kickboxing background—combined with knowledge of grappling arts like wrestling, judo and jiu-jitsu— makes anybody a real fighter.
Mike Swain

I know there are people in Brazilian jiu-jitsu who don't like to change, evolve and create new things. I am the opposite. I like to analyze and study different ways of improving whatever technique I'm doing.
Leo Vieira

If the owner of a jiu-jitsu school has an open mind, he should present or teach other styles that work well with jiu-jitsu.
Marcio Feitosa

I want to affect my students' lives every day. I want to teach and adjust the position just a little. But I also want to touch them and give them the support they need emotionally.
Carlos Valente

Fighting moves came very natural to me. I had my first degree black in taekwon-do within one year, and my black belt in kyokushin within two—which is very fast by European standards.
Bas Rutten

Don't talk bad about anyone. Train hard and focus on your own training and life.
Gokor Chivichyan

One of the most important things that you take with you in the martial arts journey is the atmosphere of the places where you train. In the long run, the techniques are important, but the environment and the memories of the other students stay with you forever.
Carlos "Caique" Elias

The submission technique is there waiting for you, but you need to know how set it up.
Fabio Santos

I became aware of the responsibility of carrying the Gracie name and of the many things expected of me.
Carlos Gracie Jr

Judo was very natural activity for me because of my grappling with my brother. What was really hard were my first days in tae kwon do training. I didn't know what I was getting into. All the kicking and punching made my body terribly sore.
Eric Paulson

I use a lot of meditation. This helps me to visualize my matches and mentally prepare to deal with the pressure of fighting. It helps me to be more focused so I can think about all the little details of the fight in a more precise way.
Frank Shamrock

At first I used all the wrestling moves that I knew, so the judo instructors would kick me out of class for using those techniques.
Gene LeBell

I also studied boxing because I realized that it would be a great complement to my previous training as far as knowing how to fight a striker.
Gokor Chivichyan

The real secret to becoming an expert in martial arts is realizing that training is a process of self-discovery.
Shizuya Sato

As a child I was always sick and very small for my age. When I attended school I used to experience fainting spells. I guess that I was very allergic to the school! The school forbade me from engaging in any kind of physical activity because the family doctor said that I was a physically deprived child.
Helio Gracie

I remember one time that I felt very bad and my brother John said to my parents, "I want to be like Jean Jacques and cut off my fingers, too, so I can be good like him." So when you hear something like that it makes you feel good about life, not just about jiu-jitsu.
Jean Jacques Machado

Punches and kicks are what I like the most, but I have also practiced jiu-jitsu, judo, and luta livre, which is Hugo Duarte's no-gi style of submission fighting. I consider myself a complete fighter.
Marco Ruas

If I go out there tomorrow and lose in the tournament there's always the next day, and the next day. The world isn't going to end.
Mark Kerr

Much of what I was doing back then is still the right thing to do. But today I would add more elbows and knees on the feet as well as the ground.
Matt Furey

I never blamed the rules for losing or winning a competition. Every fighter that steps into a ring knows the rules and has already agreed on them. So do your best and don't complain if you lose.
Oleg Taktarov

The only way of proving an art effective is putting it to the test.
Relson Gracie

The submission technique is the tip of the iceberg. You can only get the submission technique if you control the opponent at will, and the only way you can control the opponent at will is through perfect positioning.
Fabio Santos

The training at that early time under the Gracie family was very technical and very specific and detail oriented.
Renato Magno

Jiu-jitsu is a very gentle way to learn. By following its principles, you become a better person just by learning how to fight.
Rickson Gracie

I'm not going to change the things I like just for the money.
Rigan Machado

When I began teaching, although I was very young, I knew I couldn't go wrong if I followed my father's footsteps. So I used his words and told his stories—and sure enough my students loved it.
Rorion Gracie

For my first competition I was only 7 years old. My dad came to me and said, "I want you to go there and have fun. If you win I am going to give you five dollars—but if you lose I am going to give you ten dollars." So I thought, "What a deal, if I win I make a little money and get the medal, and if I lose I get even more money."
Royler Gracie

I don't just do well fighting the Gracies, I do well fighting anyone. The Gracies are just like any others for me.
Wallid Ismael

I quit Okazaki's organization because they wanted me to teach the same things he was teaching in the '20s. I didn't believe in those things anymore, because I wanted to be practical in my approach to jiu-jitsu.
Wally Jay

*After I got the purple belt, I started devoting more time to jiu-jitsu.
I got stronger and more dedicated and started doing more tournaments
and doing well in them. Wallid Ismail inspired me to devote this time
to jiu-jitsu as a purple belt and to see jiu-jitsu as a career.*
Carlos Baretto

*When a fighter is not competent using the basic and fundamental
techniques, he always tries to compensate and create new things
to cope with that. Then they criticize the basics describing them
as "old." This is a non-sense affirmation.*
Helio Gracie

*When I put myself into a fight—and I really concentrate on it—I know
that I can do well. But when my mind is not there, that is when I don't
do as well.*
Vitor Belfort

*Win or lose, I demand that my students use technique—not strength.
I demand that they use jiu-jitsu techniques that display the "jiu-jitsu
personality." There is no brutal force. That's not jiu-jitsu.*
Fabio Santos

*I have never been attracted to the more traditional martial arts systems
so I think the UFC is a great forum for those whom advocate a realistic
approach to combat sports.*
Randy Couture

Although my father was teaching all the time, he did not pressure us to participate. He was not like that.
Willy Cahill

If you can control as many factors as possible, the chances of you winning are a lot better.
Rico Chiapparelli

I believe boxing is a perfect compliment for jiu-jitsu because it teaches how to use hands effectively.
Wander Braga

Sometimes it does not matter if you beat the bully but only that you stand up to him.
Hugo Duarte

Wrestlers have great training methods and drills from which any jiu-jitsu practitioner can benefit.
Paulo Gillobel

My main strategy is to protect myself and avoid to get hit. After I covered that aspect, then I try to adapt to what my opponent gives me.
Rickson Gracie

To become really good at something requires luck and talent.
Hayward Nishioka

A good jiu-jitsu man knows how to "place" the technique on time.
Fabio Santos

When it comes to a fight, I fear no opponent. All of my training has been designed to prepare me for the ring or the streets.
Carley Gracie

My greatest joy has come from producing numerous world champions from all races and walks of life.
Carlson Gracie

I probably opened doors for some other people and brought hope for those who didn't know that it wasn't necessary to be a monster with huge muscles to defend yourself effectively.
Royce Gracie

It was a great time because everybody was together, training and working for the good of all jiu-jitsu. Carlson was teaching all the time, and I learned a lot of tactics on the ground. He knows a lot about jiu-jitsu and how to use it properly.
Fabio Gurgel

A lot of the best martial artists in the world have learned and trained at Gene's cabin. So I started grappling with Gene, and it soon became a real passion.
John Lewis

I'm grateful to my loyal students. To show my appreciation, I'm committed to teaching them the best jiu-jitsu in the world.
Cleber Luciano

In Royce Gracie's time, for example, no one knew jiu-jitsu, so it was easy to fight against opponents who had no idea what was coming. But today, everyone knows jiu-jitsu.
Rodrigo Medeiros

Today everybody does the same style of fighting—punching and kicking with some variation of jiu-jitsu. Now is not about the style, but about the athlete.
Rorion Gracie

I really like boxing, and I feel it is a very good complement to jiu-jitsu. It is an efficient art for those who want to learn to use their hands for fighting.
Helio "Soneca" Moreira

The beginning phase of any martial art sets the foundations for who and what you'll become the rest of your life.
Jason Morris

I believe that you learn a lot by having an open mind. The way I improve quickly is by copying champions. I watch what a champion does and then I try to do what he does. Then I just add my own style and flair.
B.J. Penn

When I was competing I stayed motivated because I wanted to be the best and I hated to lose. That is the only good motivation. My advice is to stay open-minded, load everything up in your mind that you see in other fights, and then use it in training.
Bas Rutten

If your base is jiu-jitsu, learn other arts to complement what you have, but don't be so naïve as to try to beat an experienced kickboxer when you have only trained stand-up for a few years.
Nino Schembri

If you never have been on the mat with Rickson Gracie, you simply don't know what Brazilian jiu-jitsu is all about!
Fabio Santos

Real budo mastery is not for everybody. The path is too hard for most people, and rewards are seldom obvious.
Shizuya Sato

The first time I knew the UFC was legitimate it was in the locker room during the first fight. Gerard Gordeau hit the sumo wrestler with a right hand and dropped him to the mat. He followed that with a roundhouse kick that hit the sumo wrestler right in the face. The sumo wrestler's front teeth went flying out of the cage and into the front rows.
Ken Shamrock

To be successful you have to have goals and work in that direction. You have to train hard and smart—otherwise everything you want will just be a dream. A goal is an impossible dream if you don't take the necessary steps to make it happen.
Carlos "Caique" Elias

I always remember my sacrifices in Japan and the hours of training each and every day included judo, running, weight training and other forms of exercise. These really built my fundamental character to be the best I can be at anything in life.
Mike Swain

If you train hard and develop a strong closed guard, you won't necessarily need to open your legs all the time and work from the open position.
Leo Vieira

To be really good in Brazilian jiu-jitsu, you have to have more dedication. The natural talent is not as important as dedication.
Marcio Feitosa

Rickson Gracie gave me my fulfillment as a fighter.
Carlos Valente

Even though kyokushinkai karate is very tough, there was no hitting to the head. So after six months or so I also started to train in Thai boxing. Three weeks after I signed up for my first class I fought my first Thai boxing match.
Bas Rutten

I have a lot of confidence in jiu-jitsu so I know I can win no matter how big the opponent may be. Technique is what is important.
Fabio Santos

If you decide to compete then you need to have a wide understanding of many techniques, although not necessarily to use them all. You need to know them and understand the way they work so you can counter them with your specialties—that is the key.
Carlos "Caique" Elias

The jiu-jitsu method my father learned was very Japanese in nature, but definitely not the modern Japanese jiu-jitsu you can see today. It was the old method that influenced the judo techniques later on. My father learned that method and modified certain aspects of what was taught to him; but it was his brother, my uncle Helio, who made great improvements in the defensive aspects of the art.

Carlos Gracie Jr

During my first boxing classes I tried to kick the guy in the stomach and the coach had to keep telling me to use my hands only to knock the guy out.

Eric Paulson

Jigoro Kano was not a very big person or in very good health, so as a young boy he studied ju-jutsu. It also afforded him an avenue of getting a sense of control over his environment.

Hayward Nishioka

Many fighters only focus on the physical part of the game, but fighting is a very mental activity, it's a psychological game. This mental aspect affects the physical component of the equation to a very high extent.

Frank Shamrock

Use anything that helps you. Don't follow the rules, break them to win. In fighting is not about how you play the game—the only thing that counts is who's standing at the end.
Gene LeBell

Boxing helped me a lot and opened my eyes as far as understanding what a properly-trained fighter can do with his hands. I guess I was right in my research instincts, because today every MMA fighter studies boxing.
Gokor Chivichyan

Sometimes I'd find myself in a situation, using the technique the way it was taught to my brother, Carlos, by the Japanese teacher. But I couldn't get it to work because the classical techniques would require a lot of strength. So I had to find a way to make it work using leverage, not muscle strength.
Helio Gracie

I prefer the stand-up fight and think it is more beautiful; nevertheless, I also like to fight on the ground.
Marco Ruas

All of a sudden the Russian judo fighters began to win international competitions because they adapted a lot of the sambo ground techniques. They also modified many of the judo grips, making everything more difficult for the orthodox judo practitioner.
Oleg Taktarov

In jiu-jitsu, submission is the only thing I ever go for. It is the reward for the art.
Jean Jacques Machado

In wrestling or boxing to be considered the best, you have to fight the best. If you don't, then it just a fantasy created and maintain by your fans and supporters. You're only the best if you fight against the best.
Mark Kerr

Even though I practice submission all the time, in a street fight I wouldn't rely on them. Face locks and chokes are good on the feet but once you hit the ground you want to end things as quickly as possible, and this is usually done with palm strikes, elbows and knees.
Matt Furey

You need to incorporate different training to be a complete MMA fighter.
Fabio Santos

I believe that the UFC has been a very revealing experience for a lot of fighters and it has opened the eyes to a lot of martial artist.
Relson Gracie

Most who idolize martial arts teachers are needy people who require a great deal of attention themselves.
Shizuya Sato

The training with the Gracie family was not competition oriented. It was very, very technical and we were not in any kind of rush to learn thousand of new movements to win a tournament. The basic were strongly emphasized and the technical level was very high.
Renato Magno

The goal is to be a well-rounded martial artist, especially when you are talking about real self-defense.
Rickson Gracie

I want to be the best teacher I can be. I want to build a good school, good students, and a good environment for everyone, regardless of where they're from.
Rigan Machado

I teach jiu-jitsu because I love it, not because I can't do anything else.
Rorion Gracie

The person with the least amount of endurance would prefer a shorter fight, and the person who is more technical prefers a longer match.
Royler Gracie

I've always thought it to be wrong when the Gracies boasted to be the only ones who could teach jiu-jitsu.
Wallid Ismael

You have to know where you're going and what you're looking for. A lot of people just cross-train for fun. That's not the goal.
Wally Jay

Only when you have a strong base, and deep understanding of the foundation of the art, can you use certain technical aspects that would be fatal if you didn't have that knowledge.
Carlos Gracie Jr

I have a guard that is hard to pass, and it is very dangerous to my opponents. I have worked hard at it, and I'm happy with my progress in that area.
Carlos Baretto

The problem is that I get bored with the sport sometimes. That is what happened to me in the past. I'm not going to blame other people for what I've done or haven't done.
Vitor Belfort

In general, if you learn 10 different martial arts styles, you will just end up being confused. If you only want to practice self-defense, there is no reason to train in anything but Brazilian jiu-jitsu.
Wander Braga

In the martial arts, people think that if you know all the moves you're going to be great, but that's meaningless to a large extent. The question is, "Can you apply those techniques in a live combat situation?"
Rico Chiapparelli

Personally, I have learned a lot about myself competing in MMA. The exposure, being in the public … it's all positive for me. The financial benefits have been fairly good as well.
Randy Couture

Training and performing while you teach is great and will keep you going but your personal training has to take you to the next level, a higher level that can't be achieved just by training with your students while you are imparting knowledge to a class. As an instructor your goal is to make your guys better and as a fighter your goal is to make yourself better.
Eric Paulson

Luta-livre is famous for being effective in foot and leg locks. They have many more leg and foot combinations than jiu-jitsu. The main difference between jiu-jitsu and luta-livre is that jiu-jitsu uses the gi and luta-livre doesn't.
Hugo Duarte

Physical talent doesn't mean anything if you don't put in time on the mat. You may be better than another guy in the first stages of the training. However, if he trains more than you, he will make you tap— regardless of your natural talent.
Paulo Gillobel

Eventually Kano became an English teacher. His ability in English afforded him opportunities to expand into international relations.
Hayward Nishioka

One day my father said that if we wanted to play football we would have to learn how to fall, which we would learn in the martial arts.
Willy Cahill

Actually, the fighters who challenged me the most were two of my own brothers. Outside of my family, the toughest fighter I encountered was Sergio Ines.
Carley Gracie

I would never prepare a fighter to face a Gracie family member in a no-holds-barred match, but everybody knows I have prepared many to fight against other Gracies in jiu-jitsu tournaments. Don't forget Wallid Ismail, who beat Royce Gracie.
Carlson Gracie

Traditional martial artists try to shy away from our sport because they normally don't fight very well.
Frank Shamrock

Physically a Japanese is much more flexible than the average European or American so in a way that should be an advantage but in reality it is not and the overall mental ability of the Europeans and Americans is much stronger than the average Japanese.
Jon Bluming

The only reason the Gracie family had to do these kind of matches was to put to test what we were developing and to prove to others that what we have works against an uncooperative opponent, regardless of the style he practices.
Royce Gracie

Nowadays, MMA is about the best man. Styles help, of course, but today you see jiu-jitsu people beating wrestlers and wrestlers beating jiu-jitsu fighters. This is because it's about individuals.
Fabio Gurgel

Because of his contacts, Dr. Kano was able to come into contact with many educators not only in Great Britain and the United States, but also throughout the world.
Hayward Nishioka

The main thing I learned in Brazilian jiu-jitsu was the smooth transition between positions and submissions. In jiu-jitsu, the smooth transition between positions is unique to the art.
John Lewis

It's very easy to train and get in shape, but you need a lot of heart to be a champion and keep it going.
Fabio Santos

My strategy in competition is to be relaxed. In all my fights, I relax and make sure in the first two or three minutes that I don't make a mistake and get behind on points.
Cleber Luciano

If a man shows you something, give him credit—even if it is only one single technique. Always give credit where credit is due.
Gokor Chivichyan

Before it was a martial art against another martial art. But that day is gone. Today it is fighter versus fighter. It is hard to find a pure jiu-jitsu guy beating everyone or a pure wrestler beating everyone or a pure puncher and kicker. Everyone cross-trains.
Rodrigo Medeiros

I have acquired the most important secrets of the art—good basics and strong fundamentals. I have seen a lot of black belts with weak and poor knowledge of the basics. This is bad for the art.
Helio "Soneca" Moreira

I learned to train smart and get the most out my time in the dojo. I try to pass this approach and mentality to my students so they can get the most of their mat time.
Jason Morris

I am not closed-minded; I am not one of those guys who says, "Jiu-jitsu is the only thing!" I don't want to stop learning; I want to learn everything … whatever I need to learn to make my game more complete.
B.J. Penn

A victory throughout a knockout is what I call an "accidental victory." Not a victory based on technique and strategy. Anyone can get knocked out with one accidental punch but it doesn't mean the opponent is better and more technical than you.
Helio Gracie

Long hours of hard training brought me confidence and self-esteem, and I used those qualities to go forward in my competition career. The only thing that can beat fear is the confidence gained from experience.
Nino Schembri

Pat Smith said to me: "I'm gonna kill you, man." It didn't mean a thing to me. I just thought, "I've seen this crap before. So what?" We got into the cage, and I finished him in less than a minute with a heel hook. It was fun.
Ken Shamrock

Judo is now a combination of many styles. However, pure technique still prevails.
Mike Swain

My advice is to stick to the basics and work hard until you can make these basics work any time and under any circumstances.
Leo Vieira

Once you have an understanding of what your opponent can do the idea is to limit the elements he can use. By doing this, his possibilities of attack and defense are restricted.
Rickson Gracie

The Gracie Barra Academy was right in front of my house. A friend of mine joined the academy, and he told me how fun it was. I started to train and that was it.
Marcio Feitosa

It is not a bad thing to learn the other aspects of combat to help you to better apply your main art.
Rorion Gracie

You must have respect and honesty. You must respect yourself and have the respect of your students.
Carlos Valente

One of the Japanese tried to hurt me during our sparring and that resulted in him going to the hospital for some stitches in his head.
Bas Rutten

You must know many different ways of using your special moves or pretty soon all your opponents will know how to stop you before you even think about trying.
Carlos "Caique" Elias

The jiu-jitsu learned by my father had all the necessary attacking components. The offensive techniques were really strong and barely needed any improvement. The old jiu-jitsu was strong on attacking techniques, but weak on defense.
Carlos Gracie Jr

Competition brings the best of me and it's under pressure that I give the best. It may be a psychological thing,

I guess.
Eric Paulson

Jiu-jitsu is an art and a sport. In any sport, sometimes you win and sometimes you lose. Therefore, be prepared for defeat, accept it and move on.
Helio "Soneca" Moreira

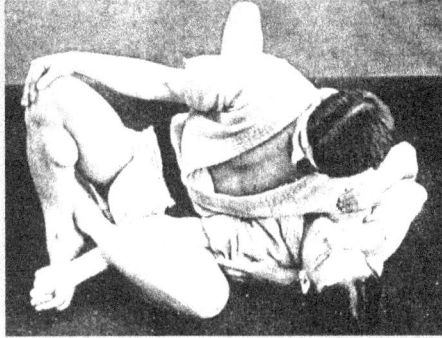

I love compete but I don't love to fight. I enjoy the competition aspect but not necessarily the fighting side of it. I know it's going to sound funny, but I'm not the kind of guy who has no problem punching people. So I really have to make an effort and visualize myself doing this.
Frank Shamrock

Dr. Kano's three maxims made judo a unique activity because it now had a philosophy rather than just movement.
Hayward Nishioka

My system is about fighting—even dirty fighting if you have to.
Gene LeBell

Spending most of my time in the dojo changed my life for the better or I could have gotten into serious trouble and ended up in jail.
Gokor Chivichyan

The martial arts—and judo especially—teach that there is no such thing as instant gratification.
Jason Morris

Due to jiu-jitsu training I began to get rid off the mental complexes that I had as a weak child. I was not insecure anymore and I became more confident and outgoing as I began teaching and helping other people to improve.
Helio Gracie

No matter where I am I'm looking for the finishing move. I learned this way and I feel that it is a very creative style.
Jean Jacques Machado

When I came to United Sates to fight in the UFC, they labeled me a grappler, when in fact I considered myself a stand-up fighter. I like to punch and kick.
Marco Ruas

Weight training is part of my training program but not as much as people think. Strength is a necessary factor in fighting.
Mark Kerr

The pro style of catch wrestling is coming back due to the work I've done, and it's a perfect example of how much has been either lost or watered down and flowed out of the knowledge base.
Matt Furey

I did open-style fighting and in order to know more about other systems and at the same time improve my arsenal I had to cross-train.
Oleg Taktarov

Understand the grappling aspect of a real fight is something very important for all martial artists.
Relson Gracie

Personally, I had to work hard in order to get better at jiu-jitsu. I know some people are very natural and able to duplicate techniques very fast, but I had to work at it.
Renato Magno

The art of jiu-jitsu is soft because it is based on the movements of leverage. It does not have brutality stamped on the movements that are used; the movements are "gentle."
Rickson Gracie

When I'm training I like to only focus on myself and use all my energy to try to improve my skills and to get the mental and physical sides of myself at 100 percent.
Rigan Machado

Month-after-month, and year-after-year I endured, until finally starting the UFC. After that everyone understood what I was talking about. It took me 25 years but I accomplished my goal.
Rorion Gracie

I have always loved fighting. After a while it becomes a natural part of your life. I live exclusively from fighting and teaching jiu-jitsu, grappling, and MMA.
Royler Gracie

I won the fight against Royce Gracie not because of luck. I won because my jiu-jitsu is a great deal superior to his.
Wallid Ismael

Kano felt that there was two kinds of judo: small judo and large judo. Large judo is using judo as a microcosm, using judo as a stepping stone or place where you can learn valuable lessons.
Hayward Nishioka

You have to go outside of your base system to gain knowledge and become more unpredictable.
Wally Jay

I like to do the guard and use that to tap out my opponent; I am most comfortable there. I love to fight from the bottom.
Carlos Baretto

Sometimes in our lives we make mistakes. When we recognize that mistakes were made, we can correct them. God gives us free will so we can do what we want. And sometimes we forget to ask God what we should be doing.

Vitor Belfort

If you are serious about MMA, you should train boxing, muay Thai or other striking arts.

Wander Braga

When my father passed away and I had the responsibilities of the school, I decided to drop out. I didn't have the energy or motivation to carry on what my father had left. However, Wally Jay came over and told me that I had to teach. He said that it was my responsibility.

Willy Cahill

Technique is one small aspect of a competition. You've also got mental toughness, fitness, attitude, et cetera. It's not unusual to see guys in the UFC with no technique beating guys with tons of technique. You can force a guy into your position and your style.

Rico Chiapparelli

Those who believe that events like the UFC are dangerous don't know what they are talking about. We are athletes, and we are well prepared to face the demands and realism of MMA fights.
Randy Couture

In the old days, actually not that long ago, jiu-jitsu players used to call us all kinds of bad names because we fought without the gi. They thought it was the stupidest thing they could imagine. Now, though, since Abu Dhabi started, they do not use the gi. It just tells us that we were right all along.
Hugo Duarte

Ultimately, the greatest benefit of all martial arts training, not only jiu-jitsu, is self-understanding. Many of the people training jiu-jitsu never try to understand their own condition or limitations. It is through jiu-jitsu training that they can get a clearer picture not only of their own physical abilities, but also of their mental limitations.
Carlos Gracie Jr

We should respect the fact that people train martial arts for different reasons and in the end it is the person who makes the style work.
Carlos "Caique" Elias

The most common mistake is thinking you are an expert striker after just a few months of training. This is just as ludicrous as an accomplished striker thinking he is an expert grappler after a few months on the mats.
John Lewis

For me, jiu-jitsu is the best because it can help you in your life. MMA events are a very small part of the whole picture.
Fabio Gurgel

There is no reason to go to the ground if you can finish the fight standing. This is particularly important in street fighting and self-defense, because you are less vulnerable to a second attacker and can leave the scene much more quickly if you are already on your feet.
Carley Gracie

It is no longer the privilege of only the Gracie family to know the best techniques.
Carlson Gracie

We prepare the situation for that technique to happen. Don't force it. Create an environment in which the technique will be there naturally.
Royce Gracie

Hard work and consistent training are more important than natural talent. Talent, without passion and dedication, means nothing.
Paulo Gillobel

Martial arts training is a pursuit that provides infinite opportunities for growth; it gives back as much as you put into it.
Shizuya Sato

I don't believe in falling back into the guard and pulling your opponent on top.
Cleber Luciano

What makes jiu-jitsu so great and what attracts people is that every martial art except jiu-jitsu has a limit.
Rodrigo Medeiros

A teacher can't teach only the movements he likes. He needs to have a complete knowledge and understanding of the art and share all its possibilities with his students.
Helio "Soneca" Moreira

The mind is a very powerful tool, and a competitor should learn how to use it and channel his thoughts in the proper direction.
Jason Morris

Many teachers out there don't fully try to make their students better than they are. If you are an honest teacher your goal has to be make your students reach a higher level than your own.
Eric Paulson

Probably one of the big things that Dr. Kano did was that he placed a big emphasis on ukemi. Ukemi is the art of falling, which enabled practitioners of judo to fall without getting hurt.
Hayward Nishioka

Now I train like a professional. You have to be committed if you want to be successful. The sport of MMA is growing in that direction.
B.J. Penn

I try to be creative and the only way I can do that is by keeping an open mind. I love to look at other competitors and grapplers and study what they do.
Nino Schembri

Royce and I were the first great rivalry of the UFC. I really think it was the thing that got fans all around the world involved in the sport.
Ken Shamrock

Jiu-jitsu and judo are close in techniques. Yet, because of the rules, they are two different games.
Mike Swain

Train the basics first because they are the foundation for everything else.
Leo Vieira

When you stop competing and fighting then you need to find a reason to keep doing it as part of your daily life. The goal, the aim of a title fight is not there so you have to re-evaluate your motives to train in martial arts and keep dragging your butt to the gym every single day.
Frank Shamrock

I believe that the biggest changes are not in techniques but in the way I face winning and losing, the way I deal with students and my instructor and the way I see life.
Marcio Feitosa

All students have to be treated the same, although everyone is on a different mission; everyone needs to feel important.
Carlos Valente

All martial arts events are positive as long as you grow and don't keep your eyes shut and deny that the old way of semi-contact and point karate is the best, because it is not. Full contact is far closer to reality and you have to change or be left behind.
Bas Rutten

You need to have a variety of ways to apply your submission techniques and keep your opponent guessing what's going to be next.
Carlos "Caique" Elias

Due to his physical limitations, Helio, who was very small and light in stature, came up with new ways of controlling the opponent and developed new strategies for the defensive aspects of jiu-jitsu. How to control a bigger and stronger opponent became the main point of the defensive maneuvers.
Carlos Gracie Jr

When I went to Japan for training I realized that at that time I was already doing the same kind of training. But after my study with the Japanese teachers everything became more systematized, more compact as far as technical structure goes. There were a lot of focus mitts drills and pads workouts.
Eric Paulson

My mental training goes parallel to the physical part but it's done mostly in private, when resting, in bed, walking, et cetera mostly between my three-times-per-day training schedule.
Frank Shamrock

Many of the old systems were effective back then because nobody knew about them. Times have changed and every street fighter knows how to deal with a front kick or a reverse punch, so the old stuff doesn't work anymore.
Gene LeBell

I met Gene LeBell and showed him how we trained in Armenia. We shared some thoughts and finally said, "What you are doing is good, but I'll teach you how to fight like a man!" Needless to say, I found out that I was missing something!
Gokor Chivichyan

When you are more confident and secure, you become much more tolerant of others because you don't need to prove yourself. It clears your mind to concentrate on other things.
Helio Gracie

In order to get a good finish, of course, you should have some type of control of the other person. Control can also mean forcing the person into a position where you know how they're going to react.
Jean Jacques Machado

The truth is that I have nothing against jiu-jitsu and have great friends who train jiu-jitsu. I respect this style of fighting, I practice it and I think it is very good and very efficient.
Marco Ruas

When you are stronger than your opponent you can get away from many situations and balance your lack of technique. But technique just by itself is useless, you need a certain amount of strength to help.
Mark Kerr

I never practiced jiu-jitsu with the popularity and money goals in mind. I never cared about it. My only objective was to make the art better and make myself better to better protect myself.
Helio Gracie

Judo isn't what it used to be. Hate to say it, but the Olympics basically ruined real judo.
Matt Furey

Japan's model has always been that of technique. The Japanese believe that it is the technique that is going to save the day.
Hayward Nishioka

Only if you know your opponent's game can you fight him and win.
Oleg Taktarov

Grappling is very subtle and requires an educated spectator to fully understand what the fighters are doing or trying to do.
Relson Gracie

There weren't many jiu-jitsu competitions so the focus was more on self-defense. The training was very quality-oriented and the sportive aspect was not fully developed.
Renato Magno

Good jiu-jitsu doesn't use strength, it doesn't have to be brutal. Jiu-jitsu is supposed to be a beautiful art. It's a matter of skill.
Rickson Gracie

To know how to punch and kick is great, but we can't close our eyes to the most crucial aspect of a real fight—which is that 95 percent of all fights end up on the ground.
Rorion Gracie

I don't believe that anyone will tell you that they love to fight NHB. People may love the attention and the exposure and the perks, but no one in his right mind likes to hit someone or to get hit in a fight.
Royler Gracie

The only way you can be confident of what you know is to have strong technical fundamentals.
Helio "Soneca" Moreira

I fought Renzo for an hour. It was an unbelievable match. He remained under me like a child, not able to move! There were no rounds and I scored 12 and he nothing.
Wallid Ismael

With the gi, the submission game is much more technical. When you wear the gi, you have many more chances to catch your opponent.
Rigan Machado

To become your best, you cannot stay locked in your system—you cannot confine yourself to only one system. You have to study different things and find out the best way they might work for you.
Wally Jay

Although your main goal is still take your opponent down and defeat him on the ground, you need an understanding of the punching and kicking techniques because you need to know how to counters these aspects of combat.
Rickson Gracie

In sport jiu-jitsu, the guard is looser. It's a relaxed game. In MMA, the technique has to be more objective and more offensive. You can't wait for your opponent to make a mistake.
Carlos Baretto

You have to sweat for many years to be a good fighter. There are no shortcuts. You have to pay your dues, my friend. Nothing happens overnight.
Fabio Santos

Everybody must do according to the way he sees the art and how to apply to his dojo and is the best for his students.
Jon Bluming

The techniques we use today are not weaker or worse than those used in the past. The athletes are simply different and different things work now.
Jason Morris

You have to be humble and not think that you're the best. A true champion is one who doesn't think he is the best, but yet others do.
Vitor Belfort

If you are a jiu-jitsu man, though, don't step into the ring and try to kickbox with a kickboxer! Stick to what you know best and what you've been practicing.
Wander Braga

We need to look at other sports and analyze how they train. There are a lot of judo guys who work out, but they do not train. And that is a big difference.
Willy Cahill

Martial arts is not only about winning a championship or beating someone up, but rather about making friends and developing good relationships with everybody. That's the real meaning of the martial arts.
Carlos "Caique" Elias

But then I saw the Gracies and I thought, "You know, there's something to that stuff." I always kind of rolled across my back in wrestling, but I would never stay there.
Rico Chiapparelli

Mr. Inokuma credits Donn Draeger as having helped him to have the strength that most other judo players may not have had. No one else was really weight training in judo before that time.
Hayward Nishioka

The training approach has changed drastically; kickboxing, grappling, wrestling, etc. have come together to create a format that is used by all of us.
Randy Couture

It makes me proud to think that luta-livre stood up to jiu-jitsu for all those years, and now jiu-jitsu is copying us.
Hugo Duarte

You have to learn to be patient and understand that the good things take time. In any sport or activity, excellence won't happen overnight, and jiu-jitsu is no exception.
Paulo Gillobel

Once my father had learned traditional jiu-jitsu from the Japanese point of view, he adapted it to a more practical style for street fighting.
Carley Gracie

If you fight a boxer, you better know how to slip a punch or you're going to get nailed. Being successful in jiu-jitsu is as much about being open-minded to learning new things as it is about learning a particular set of techniques.
Carlson Gracie

Judo is mostly a game these days, and our approach to fighting is different. Jiu-jitsu is not about sport, and we are not judo players.
Royce Gracie

You can't educate kids with no-holds-barred events, but you can help kids with jiu-jitsu.
Fabio Gurgel

If you are a strong stand-up striker, it is extremely advisable to learn as much about ground techniques as possible … if for nothing more than to know how to defend your weaknesses and keep or bring the fight back to your feet where your strengths lie.
John Lewis

Brazilian jiu-jitsu has a good reputation as a combat method. We don't need to do crazy things to prove that anymore, because everybody knows it.
Carlos Gracie Jr

If you work for two or three minutes, you can get your opponent a little tired and confused. When you subsequently get the position you want, you have a much better chance of your attacks working.
Cleber Luciano

Jiu-jitsu is infinite; anyone can teach you a new move.
Rodrigo Medeiros

It is the instructor's responsibility to give all his knowledge to the students. If a teacher saves a little here and there, eventually it will weaken the art.
Helio "Soneca" Moreira

I don't know what Kano intended when he created judo because I never met him, but it has developed into one of the most dynamic sports in the world.
Jason Morris

I always push myself to train harder than my students. Maybe this is a residual attitude of my professional days. I use a lot of the training aspects and methodology that I use with my students in my personal training.
Eric Paulson

Train hard and practice the martial arts for fun. If you don't enjoy it, you are never going to be any good at it.
B.J. Penn

The simple training can bring you a lot of joy and pleasure without getting involved in any type of combat. You can take from martial arts what is good for you.
Frank Shamrock

My goal in teaching was always to teach my students to be able of defeating me, because when they got better, they pushed me harder and I had to get better too.
Helio Gracie

To develop your own game, you have to find what really works for you based on your physical characteristics.
Nino Schembri

Royce Gracie didn't move on because the rules changed. He moved on because the competition was getting tough, and everyone was learning his game.
Ken Shamrock

Any time you step into a fighting ring you challenge yourself and become a stronger person for trying, regardless if you win or lose.
Mike Swain

We all know the same techniques, but we spice them up with a personal approach that gives each game an individual flavor.
Leo Vieira

I win when I overcome myself and I lose when I stop and see my limits.
Marcio Feitosa

As an instructor, it's almost like I'm a diplomat. I get to know people all over the world. I get to know police officers, dentists. It is tremendous.
Carlos Valente

Always look for the principle that makes a technique work. If you can determine what the principle is, than you will be able to learn the technique better.
Shizuya Sato

Everything changes and uses new ideas to improve—human languages add news words, cars get more horsepower, tennis players hit harder, and runners move faster. The same thing is true with martial arts. We now all think that mixed martial arts is the best way to fight, but that could change too. Only God knows what's next.
Bas Rutten

You must have a complete game and develop an understanding of the advantageous positions and how to get into them—because regardless of the instructor's approach, the principles and concepts involved in maintaining and escaping from each of the main positions are universal.
Carlos "Caique" Elias

Helio proved through all his vale tudo fights that the jiu-jitsu developed by the Gracie family had the tools to control and defeat bigger opponents, wearing them down and putting them into submission.
Carlos Gracie Jr

I'm a counter-fighter by nature, so learning how to wait for the opponent to attack me was my main interest. I let the guy come close to punch me, kick me or trying to take me down and then it is when I reverse the situation and I come up on top.
Eric Paulson

Confidence is one of the most important mental components in a fighter. No confidence in yourself and you are done. You don't want to be unsure of your abilities because that is going to be a very heavy weight during the fight. You want to be confident but not over-confident.
Frank Shamrock

Grappling is just a word for me because I use boxing, karate, savate, jiu-jitsu, wrestling, aikido, sambo, tire iron, engine transmission, et cetera.
Gene LeBell

I never enjoyed the martial arts as much as I did after I met Gene LeBell. He makes working-out fun because he is always joking and that relaxes you so you can learn more.
Gokor Chivichyan

The Gracie Challenge was a way of improving our system and letting the people see how good the techniques were. It was not a personal thing, or an ego trip.
Helio Gracie

To me the only true proof of how good you are is to finish by submission. It is the true measure of the art.
Jean Jacques Machado

It is not smart to fight in an anything-goes match without knowing anything about ground styles. I like stand-up fighting but I also know how to fight on the ground.
Marco Ruas

Strength without conditioning is useless. If you can put together technique, strength and cardiovascular conditioning, you are meant to do something important. It's like a tripod, you need the three legs together to constitute the real base to grow.
Mark Kerr

Elite competition, such as the Olympic Games, requires a highly sophisticated approach to training and psychology.
Jason Morris

Brazilian jiu-jitsu is mostly a spin-off of old-school judo, but only the groundwork portion of it.
Matt Furey

Everybody makes innovations to what they are practicing or teaching compared to what they learned in the past. Even all the great martial arts masters did. Who thinks Jigoro Kano, Gichin Funakoshi or Morihei Ueshiba taught exactly what was passed on to them by their teachers?
Oleg Taktarov

Many people don't realize that proper breathing and relaxation comes from a state of mind in which you are confident with your jiu-jitsu skills.
Helio "Soneca" Moreira

The Brazilian jiu-jitsu practitioner uses leverage and body positioning above everything else. This is the only way of making the art work against bigger opponents.
Relson Gracie

*Competitors need
to spend time catching-up
with the new competition
movements and can't
spend hours and hours
on the basics. It's very
hard to find a good
balance if the student's
interest is in competition.*
Renato Magno

*There is only one
jiu-jitsu in Brazil.
It was all created by my family. Some have a bit more technique, others
have less, but basically it's the same thing.*
Rickson Gracie

*A proper submission, whether it is an arm lock, knee bar, or whatever,
is all a result of a proper opening and that is where the gi is most helpful.*
Rigan Machado

*The Gracie Challenge had the objective of demonstrating the effectiveness
of what we teach. I owed it to all my students. It was the only way to
prove my point.*
Rorion Gracie

*Fighting is something that traumatizes the body and it not something
that I believe anyone would realistically do just for the pleasure of it.*
Royler Gracie

I am a jiu-jitsu fighter and I fight for Carlson Gracie. While his family has tried to hide his name, I have always tried to bring the name Carlson Gracie to the forefront.
Wallid Ismael

Constant change, improvement and evolution is the hallmark of a truly great martial artist.
Wally Jay

You can get hurt from the guard—especially if you're fighting a really strong wrestler with a good base. Strength does matter and so does size in MMA.
Carlos Baretto

When my mind is not there for a fight, Vitor is not there and anything can happen. And that is what happened in the first Randy Couture fight and the Sakuraba fight.
Vitor Belfort

I look for a way to defeat my opponent without unnecessary violence. I'd rather use jiu-jitsu to do that than punch the guy until the end.
Rickson Gracie

Having talent and being gifted physically only means so much. You may have all the physical ability in the world, but if you don't sweat on the mat every day you won't become a champion.
Wander Braga

Muscular strength is one of the most important requirements for developing efficient expertise in judo.
Willy Cahill

Logically, if you're going to learn anything as a wrestler, submission seems like the last one percent of wrestling because it is all the stuff that is illegal in wrestling—the joint locks, the chokes, et cetera.
Rico Chiapparelli

The first thing a fighter should do is find a style he is comfortable with. He needs to create a base on which to build everything.
Randy Couture

I believe that Rickson's technique is an unquestionable matter. I have fought against him, and I have fought against many of the people who say they are better than him. I can tell you that they just don't know. Anybody who knows anything knows that he is very technical.
Hugo Duarte

Now we have a bigger tactical arsenal but a lot of people lack the basic foundation that helps to reach the higher levels of the art.
Paulo Gillobel

I believe that the martial arts are about fighting, not fantasy. The purpose of our style of jiu-jitsu is to prepare students to defend themselves in the streets, as well as in the ring.
Carley Gracie

*People talk sometimes
because they don't have
enough important things
to do. Of course, everybody
is entitled to express an
opinion, regardless if that
opinion is based on facts
or a stupid affirmation.*
Royce Gracie

*The technical evolution of jiu-jitsu techniques is based on sport
competition. Many people criticize sport jiu-jitsu, but they never
participated in a competition.*
Fabio Gurgel

*There are certain things that you can only learn from stepping into the
cage. My biggest lesson was that no single technique or strategy works
best in cage fighting. You have to be flexible and adaptable.*
John Lewis

*Respect for other styles is very important—even if you don't agree with
their approach to combat you should respect them and not criticize
them. Without respect there is nothing.*
Carlos "Caique" Elias

*It is very easy to write and talk 'trash' but it's impossible to find one of
these cowards that show up and tell things to your face so you can get
back to them with you fist. Talk is cheap and the internet help to make
even cheaper!*
Jon Bluming

My techniques are effective in MMA fighting, so I don't have a lot of problems transferring them over. But kicking and punching do add a lot more dimension to the grappling game.
Cleber Luciano

If you are a black belt and stop training in jiu-jitsu, your techniques will get old and be out of date in three or four years. Some new move is always coming.
Rodrigo Medeiros

If you really know the art, you are not afraid of giving knowledge to students. But I don't agree with giving tons of information to a student too early, because confusion is the only result you'll get!
Helio "Soneca" Moreira

Sport was developed to compare relative skills on a level playing field. This is the reason why there are weight classes in jiu-jitsu, boxing, karate, taekwondo, judo, et cetera. We do it to level the playing field. From a sportive point of view it is simply logical. It is a combat sport, not a real self-defense situation.
Carlos Gracie Jr

The art you train in display in some way your mentality as individual.
Eric Paulson

I have always been all about the sport of judo. I love athletics and categorize judo as I would baseball, tennis or any other sport.
Jason Morris

For MMA, you really have to have an open mind. Brazilian jiu-jitsu is great, but you need to learn everything. If you come from a striking martial art, you need to learn jiu-jitsu.
B.J. Penn

Find out how your own body moves—what your strong and weak points are—and then develop a game that works specifically for you.
Nino Schembri

The MMA game has so completely changed now that if you go in knowing only one thing you're at a huge disadvantage before the bell ever sounds.
Ken Shamrock

To become a champion in the sport of judo, you must understand that judo is about making your character stronger through tough physical and mental practice on the mat.
Mike Swain

It's extremely important to have a partner you enjoy working with, someone you get along with. As a fighter both winning and losing can be very motivational, it just depends how you approach victory and defeat.

Frank Shamrock

When you start competing, your jiu-jitsu becomes more streamlined and direct. You start using only those things that really work.

Leo Vieira

If the only thing a practitioner sees in jiu-jitsu are the techniques and the only goal is the medal in the last match, he will not have the determination, discipline and strength to train in jiu-jitsu his entire life.

Marcio Feitosa

Martial arts techniques are just not there anymore. Now it's just two guys throwing each other down and pounding away. I feel that in the end that's going to affect the way the sport of MMA is perceived by the fans and hurt its popularity.

Bas Rutten

Jiu-jitsu has always been a self-defense system, not a sport. As a self-defense method the practitioner has to rely on those techniques that do not require a lot of strength and physical power to be effective.

Carlos "Caique" Elias

My father Carlos Gracie, was much older than his younger brother Helio, so it was Helio who went out and fought against anyone who doubted the effectiveness of Brazilian jiu-jitsu.
Carlos Gracie Jr

I'm not a 100% offensive fighter. I like to counter my opponent actions so I can use my own strong techniques on him.
Eric Paulson

When you lose a fight, don't blame anyone else but yourself. Go back home and work harder than before. Do your homework so "they" won't have a reason to declare your opponent victorious.
Frank Shamrock

You need to have a good base and then expand on it. It takes a high IQ and an open mind.
Gene LeBell

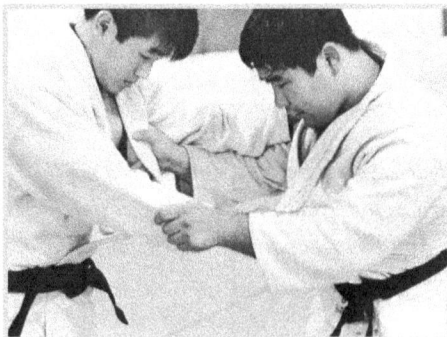

Having natural talent doesn't mean anything if you don't back it up with dedication and hours of hard work.
Gokor Chivichyan

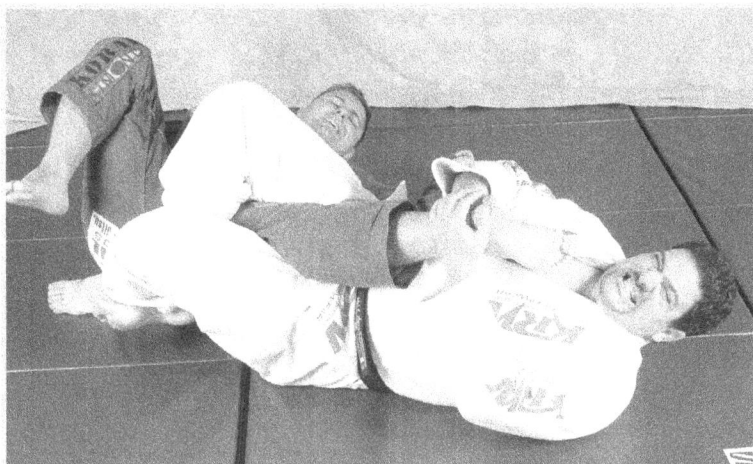

Kimura was considered "the toughest man who ever lived," at that time. He heard about me and decided that he wanted to fight me. I said, "Fine, let's go."
Helio Gracie

After training so much, your body and mind develop their own reactions. When you train grappling, which I have been doing all my life, you pretty much feel all the reactions that are possible in a given situation.
Jean Jacques Machado

Vale tudo existed only inside Brazil until the moment Rorion Gracie launched the Ultimate Fighting Championship in the U.S.
Marco Ruas

A flexibility program will help you to be more relaxed, more supple and quicker. It also helps to get rid of a lot of toxins in your body.
Mark Kerr

People tend to think that what we know today is more advanced than what the old-timers knew, but that's sort of like a 13-year-old who first discovers sex. He actually believes that he and his buddies learned something new. He's sure that his mom and dad don't know. But he's wrong.
Matt Furey

Innovations should be made based on realistic and functional experiences, otherwise they become a waste of time.
Oleg Taktarov

Of course, a certain amount of strength is necessary but the efficiency of the techniques developed by my father don't require a great deal of muscle to make them work.
Relson Gracie

I've breathed jiu-jitsu since the day I began to understand myself as a person.
Rickson Gracie

You have to find what fits you and what you're compatible with.
Wally Jay

There is only one jiu-jitsu, Brazilian jiu-jitsu. There is no difference between Brazilian and Gracie jiu-jitsu.
Wallid Ismael

Repetition is the magic that makes us strong and physically able to perform a technique. Almost nothing in the martial arts is possible without repetition.
Shizuya Sato

When you don't have the gi, you have to use a lot of speed and strength. It is not so much a technical match as it is a physical match—many of the techniques are either limited or completely eliminated.
Rigan Machado

If you teach any subject you should be able to demonstrate your knowledge. In the world of martial arts, knowledge equals effectiveness—which in turn gives you confidence.
Rorion Gracie

I learned from watching and absorbing the experience of many champions, and not just those from my own family.
Royler Gracie

A jiu-jitsu fighter must enter in a competition to win, not to compete. Today the people fight in competitions to not lose, and that's embarrassing for the art.
Helio Gracie

Regardless if your jiu-jitsu is more based on the old traditional techniques, or its focus is on modern competition, there is hardly ever an instructor who will not alter his methods to some extent.
Renato Magno

I use boxing and muay Thai as a regular part of my training. I'm also emphasizing wrestling takedowns and judo throws. Then I use jiu-jitsu for submissions.
Carlos Baretto

I respect everybody so I think that people should respect me. Some fighters are just too cocky. I don't see cockiness as a sign of confidence; I see cockiness as a sign of fear. When you have fear, you're cocky. When you're confident, you're humble.
Vitor Belfort

Strangely enough, those who quit in the early stages of training, after only a couple of years, are the ones who have the best natural ability for the sport!
Wander Braga

My technique is based on my opponent. I try to stay in what I call the "zero zone." From there, I'm ready to read what the opponent gives me to react.
Rickson Gracie

Skill, proper budo (martial way) attitude, and theoretical and practical knowledge are all indispensable in the study of the martial arts.
Willy Cahill

I finally got around to checking out Renzo Gracie's school. But Renzo wasn't there; Craig Kukuk was there. He had a really bad back so I was just watching him teach. I could tell from watching how he positioned himself that he knew what he was talking about.
Rico Chiapparelli

Wrestling was my base. From there, I went to boxing and then jiu-jitsu. I mainly wanted jiu-jitsu for the submissions and to learn how to pass the guard.
Randy Couture

Rickson is much more than just an empty reputation. Rickson is the leader of jiu-jitsu, and I am the leader of luta-livre, so a fight between us would generate a lot of interest and be very successful. I would be willing to fight for free just to see it happen.
Hugo Duarte

Evolution is good as long as we don't forget who we are and from where we came.
Paulo Gillobel

The martial artist must be physically strong because all technique is based on movement of the body.
Shizuya Sato

*I believe it's better to learn three things well than to know a little
bit about a lot of things. One well-executed move can finish a fight,
but many poorly-done moves will get you nowhere.*
Carley Gracie

*Rorion was the mastermind behind the UFC and the Gracie revolution
in the United States. I simply did what I have been doing all my life.
I stepped into the ring and fought.*
Royce Gracie

*If you are not willing to change, you are going to lose. This applies
not only to jiu-jitsu but to everything in life, including business.
Anyone running a business for more than 10 years knows that changes
have to be made to adapt to changing market situations.*
Fabio Gurgel

*The success of our team doesn't come from making a generic mold that
I try to fit all my students into. It comes from my ability to recognize
and build on people's individual talents.*
John Lewis

*If you lock somebody in the closed guard but then only defend from it,
you are going to have problems.*
Cleber Luciano

*Personality and technical ability are inseparable, and by practicing
technique we learn about ourselves.*
Hayward Nishioka

I tell my students that they are thinking small if they are taking jiu-jitsu to beat someone in a fight. Jiu-jitsu is for life ... it teaches you how to treat people.
Rodrigo Medeiros

A good teacher knows how much information should be given at any point in training, so the student can naturally absorb all the technical knowledge.
Helio "Soneca" Moreira

Judo practice definitely brings many mental and spiritual benefits, but the student has to look for those to find them. It has to be a personal journey.
Jason Morris

To be a total fighter, you need to learn how to strike, grapple and wrestle to be ready for both the ground and the stand-up game. Be ready for anything and never give up.
B.J. Penn

You need many years of hard training and experience in the basics before you can really understand what works for you. It takes years to find that out.
Nino Schembri

Developing strength of character is a natural result of correct training.
Shizuya Sato

Without a doubt, Erik Paulson is one of the most knowledgeable trainers in the world when it comes to combining different aspects of fighting into an integrated game.
Ken Shamrock

Every time you teach a basic movement to a beginner, you learn something new about the technique. It is an interesting process that I recommend to all those who are truly interested in reaching the higher levels of understanding in judo.
Mike Swain

In MMA, a simple wild punch can finish the fight. In a grappling competition like Abu Dhabi, you have to be technical or you will lose your first match.
Leo Vieira

They need to understand that jiu-jitsu goes much further. It is a metaphor of life. Inside the dojo, they have all the teaching/guidance they will need for life.
Marcio Feitosa

Traditional martial arts are from the East but right now the West has many world champions in every martial art. Still, it is very special to go to Asia and see the people there compete in their own styles. The East has this special feeling.
Bas Rutten

Don't let anyone steal your dreams or take your attention away from your goals, because those dreams are pretty much all you've got.
Helio "Soneca" Moreira

The overall idea is to allow the student to train as hard as possible without getting injured, while still maintaining the effectiveness necessary to defend himself on the street.
Carlos "Caique" Elias

A small jiu-jitsu man will defeat a bigger opponent who doesn't have the same jiu-jitsu knowledge, but if the bigger man is also good at jiu-jitsu then that's another story.
Carlos Gracie Jr

If a proven technique does not work for us, we must deepen out study of it until it does.
Hayward Nishioka

Shooto Instructor Yori Nakamura said to me that my body was perfect for grappling, that my physical structure was ideal for grappling arts.
Eric Paulson

Sometimes, losing can be the best thing that can happen to you. It's tough to lose, but if you do lose, make sure it doesn't happen again.
Frank Shamrock

Judo is a sport that adapts with the times and grows and improves.
Jason Morris

Every style has certain weaknesses, and every fighter has different weaknesses. You have to find out what the are and then use them to your advantage.
Gene LeBell

The only way to become a champion is to put in many hours of hard training without holding anything back. There is no other way, no short-cuts.
Gokor Chivichyan

In Japan, they have a tradition that the top guy doesn't fight challengers unless they defeat his best student. So I had to fight Kato, who was Kimura's top student and 40 pounds heavier than me.
Helio Gracie

My fighting style is well-known by everybody in jiu-jitsu—I'm always looking for a finish. Even if I don't win the match, they will know that they almost lost to me by submission.
Jean Jacques Machado

After having learned so many styles of fighting, I didn't think it was fair for me to participate to the UFC under the label of just one fighting art. In reality, my style is a mixture of many styles. That's how Ruas Vale Tudo was created.
Marco Ruas

The food is the fuel of your body. Basically you need to find out what works for you.
Mark Kerr

MMA events may have "destroyed" the idea of the one deadly punch for a lot of people, but one good punch can still be deadly as hell.
Matt Furey

I went to some Brazilian jiu-jitsu schools to help them with leg locks, but some of the instructors were not very receptive to being shown leg locks.
Oleg Taktarov

Using intelligence, leverage and body positioning is the key of Gracie jiu-jitsu.
Relson Gracie

In the end, the art of teaching is the sum total learned from theory and practice.
Renato Magno

Jiu-jitsu has given me everything I need: not only recognition, not only money, not only health and dignity, but everything I need as a man.
Rickson Gracie

I keep myself from getting too comfortable with one way of training, because then you stop learning.
Rigan Machado

Gracie jiu-jitsu enables you look at that big guy as if he were the child.
Rorion Gracie

I never lost confidence in myself but some people thought I did. My game is to sometimes play tricks on the other fighter.
Vitor Belfort

Long experience in martial arts practice will show us that our real competition is with ourselves.
Shizuya Sato

There is not a top-level fighter today who doesn't have BJJ knowledge. Likewise the world of stand-up fighting has made BJJ practitioners look to develop skills that complement their style as well.
Royler Gracie

Each art has its strong and weak points so you have to analyze those and see whether the art fits you or not. You can't train a St. Bernard to run. Well you can, but he'll never be a greyhound—it doesn't matter what training method you use.
Wally Jay

Carlson Gracie is an intelligent and open-minded man with a lot of experience in no-holds-barred. He realizes that you must mix styles and that there is no more space for a specialist in the martial arts fighting world.
Carlos Baretto

Scoring points is part of the game of sport BJJ but I believe that submissions really exemplify the true essence of the art.
Wander Braga

In sport judo as practiced today, there can be no doubt strength and conditioning play a significant part in the outcome.
Willy Cahill

The "art" within the martial arts means the ability to practice self-control and to think within yourself. No matter how difficult a situation is, or how bad it may appear to be, you have the power to control yourself.
Carlos "Caique" Elias

There's no ego in wrestling if you're wrestling with guys on your team. But Brazilian jiu-jitsu is a lot different than wrestling.
Rico Chiapparelli

In MMA, a fighter needs to know how to use his hands in every grappling situation. Unlike a grappler who looks to resolve the situation with a grappling movement, in MMA a fighter can use his hands to facilitate the escape.
Randy Couture

Injuries will come very easily if you don't train wisely, and these injuries will slow your progress.
Paulo Gillobel

As a teacher I have to explain clearly the principles of the techniques in a way that people can understand.
Carley Gracie

All positions are important. You should not concentrate on just one thing and neglect another.
Carlson Gracie

I give all the credit in the world to Wallid for what he did, but I wasn't focused enough or angry enough. And that was my mistake.
Royce Gracie

The basic movements of jiu-jitsu are the ones everybody should use and apply. The new techniques are mostly the product of high-level champions.
Fabio Gurgel

The martial arts should be more than having the ability to beat someone up.
John Lewis

All jiu-jitsu instructors should try to teach the art in the right way, emphasizing the basics and fundamentals that will allow the practitioner to evolve in their future years.
Carlos Gracie Jr

The key is to be active from the guard; you have to have mobile hips, legs and feet.
Cleber Luciano

When you're a competitor, you always want to come up with a surprise to gain an advantage. But the basic parts of jiu-jitsu are always the same.
Rodrigo Medeiros

*If a teacher doesn't want the students to learn, all he has to do is give
a lot of technical information in a random way. This will confuse the
student but nobody will be able to blame the instructor for not giving
information.*
Helio "Soneca" Moreira

*A judo player entering a MMA ring is almost the same as a tennis
player entering a basketball court. The no-holds-barred arena is its
own thing and judo is its own thing; they are two separate and
distinctive activities.*
Jason Morris

*When I train fighters I do the same way but focus more on the specific
of their individual strengths and weakness. It's the same training method
but the approach and the structure of the sessions are a little bit
different.*
Eric Paulson

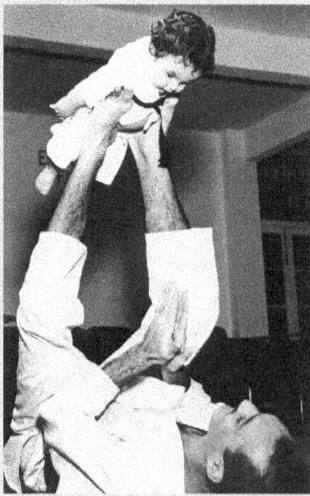

*You need to work hard for many
years before you can truly say that
a certain technique is not good
for you. At that point you'll have
the understanding to develop and
create your own movements.*
Nino Schembri

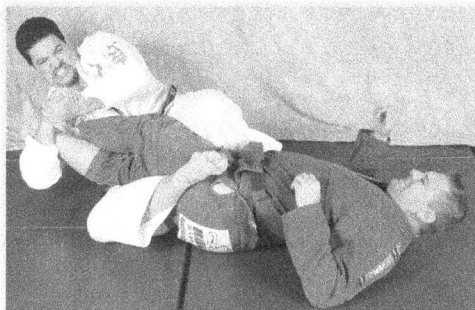

Royce is very good. No doubt about it. But his other big problem is that he still doesn't have the power he needs to fight top strikers.
Ken Shamrock

Cross-training is great when properly done; it keeps things fresh for the fighters and students. Just make sure your core techniques in the sport come before any other type of training.
Mike Swain

Jiu-jitsu is more than a simple sport. It has a certain philosophy to its practice. It can be used as a sport, but the right jiu-jitsu training develops more than the practitioner's body.
Leo Vieira

I truly believe that if you have the right kind of food you don't need to rely on supplements. But I also understand that something you can't get the right food at the right time so supplements can help to balance your nutritional intake to a certain extent.
Frank Shamrock

When you go to a dojo, you want the atmosphere to be good for you. You want to feel that the philosophy inside of the school is good for you. Techniques are only one part of the school.
Marcio Feitosa

People who say martial arts fighting is barbaric are totally wrong. Guys who say that they don't like fighting or don't want to be a good fighter not being honest with themselves.
Bas Rutten

Today jiu-jitsu is both a self-defense art and a sport. Brazilian jiu-jitsu meets both those requirements. It is not a martial arts system that hides behind a veil of mysticism, but instead deals with the realities of combat with no exaggerated claims.
Carlos "Caique" Elias

Vale tudo was created by my father, Carlos Gracie. The only reason he did it was to prove to everybody that the art of the Gracie family was an effective system of fighting.
Carlos Gracie Jr

There is a major danger in leg locks and it is that when you feel the pain, it's already too late. You are injured. They are very dangerous moves because the fighter thinks the leg can take it and all of a sudden with feeling a "progressive degree of pain," your knee pops and you have a problem.
Eric Paulson

When the fight is getting close, I try to relax as much as I can. Only right before the fight I feel a little bit nervous but I focus on my breathing and relaxation techniques as I replay in my mind all the things I visualized for week about the upcoming fight.
Frank Shamrock

If you're fighting a boxer you know his system has no defense below the waist, so you tackle him to the ground or kicking low to the legs. This way you play your game, not his.
Gene LeBell

The training methods are different, the techniques are constantly evolving, and new movements are being created all the time. You need to find a way to adapt to the ever-changing flow of things.
Gokor Chivichyan

I choked Kato into unconsciousness. All the Japanese were shocked because no foreigner had ever defeated a Japanese jiu-jitsu champion before. So that gave me the chance to fight Kimura.
Helio Gracie

I don't have four fingers on my left hand, but I was born like that. And I had to learn how to deal with it.
Jean Jacques Machado

If you really want to be a successful fighter you need a combination of different elements and systems. You have to incorporate techniques from different arts.
Marco Ruas

You need to understand how your body recovers after a hard training session or competition and how you have to nourish it.
Mark Kerr

Ultimately, it is each individual fighter that determines the outcome of a bout. Who gives a damn about which system is more advanced or not?
Matt Furey

After the first UFC I adapted and found ways to make my techniques work under those new circumstances.
Oleg Taktarov

I don't mind teaching people the jiu-jitsu techniques and secrets. Why should I? I'm very happy sharing a great self-defense system with everybody who wants to learn it.
Relson Gracie

If you are not interested in sport competition then you have to train differently, maybe with a more traditional approach.
Renato Magno

I always try to do my best and I always believe everybody has value. I respect everyone; my honor is more important than my body.
Rickson Gracie

The only reason why a person takes on the attitude of a bully is because deep down they are an insecure individual.
Rorion Gracie

Training for me is part of my life, the thing that I try to do is to adapt my lifestyle depending on what I am training for.
Royler Gracie

You can't just concentrate on one thing. You have to be able to do it all. Everyone knows what is coming now, and most fighters know a little of everything. So you have to prepare for everything.
Carlos Baretto

Talking trash is not my style. I don't need to impress anyone. I have done a lot of things in the sport and people know what I can do.
Vitor Belfort

There are a lot of things that money can buy, but let me tell you that it won't buy courage and passion for something. You can fight hard for money but there always will be a limit— a line you won't trespass simply for money.
Helio Gracie

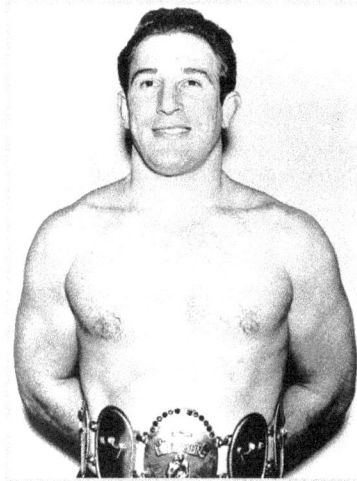

I look at jiu-jitsu as an extension of life. In life you don't stop growing and learning new things.
Wander Braga

Within any style there are millions of different approaches and interpretations. That's the way it is in any sport, not just in the martial arts.
Rico Chiapparelli

The strikes change the whole perception of the game, regardless how good your opponent is on the ground.
Randy Couture

Some instructors are afraid to teach their students short cuts and ways of being better than they are. I truly don't understand why they act that way but I assume they are afraid of their students and their behavior is not more than a reflection of their own insecurities not only in martial arts but in life as well.
Eric Paulson

Some teachers send their students to fight too soon because they want to become championship trainers, but they don't realize that you can't do that unless you truly prepare your students.
Paulo Gillobel

The fights back then did not have time limits and there were no rounds. It was a whole different ballgame, to say the least.
Royce Gracie

If you are not a full-time competitor, stick to the basics. You'll be surprised how good you can perform.
Fabio Gurgel

Find a teacher who can help you develop your mind and heart, as well as your physical skills. A strong mind and good heart will take you a long way in your life.
John Lewis

Training with a gi gives you more possibilities as far as techniques are concerned. You have more choices for choking, getting an arm-lock or controlling your opponent.
Rickson Gracie

Every time you go into a fight you should worry about yourself—not your opponent. Your goal is to fight the fight, not fight the opponent.
Cleber Luciano

Jiu-jitsu is an art that evolves constantly. New movements and technical changes appear all the time. This is good because it makes the technical aspects of the art grow constantly.
Helio "Soneca" Moreira

Once you find yourself in a position where you can't overcome an opponent because he is younger and stronger, that is when the real and authentic jiu-jitsu will come out. This usually only occurs when you can't rely on strength and power because you are not that young anymore.
Carlos Gracie Jr

There is not one style or grappling method that will make you a good student or instructor. There may be an instructor teaching judo and another teaching BJJ. If the student is dedicated and motivated, the final quality of the product (student) will be the same.
Jason Morris

A professional fighter does fight, but he does it in the ring with proper rules and respect for his opponent—not in the street.
Nino Schembri

When you fight for honor or because your life is at stake, you can do things that you'll never do for money—you can endure punishment that no money will make you to.
Helio Gracie

First develop strong basics and fundamentals. Then you can build upon that and add elements that help to improve certain technical areas of your game.
Mike Swain

I don't want to sound religious, but the deeper aspects of any martial art bring a certain spiritual meaning and benefit to the student's life outside the academy.
Leo Vieira

If you don't train smart, you can train really hard for one day. If you train smart, you can train really hard for 100 years.
Marcio Feitosa

When it comes to training I am a pretty simple guy. When something works for me, I won't change it.
Bas Rutten

MMA is a completely different game than a real fight. In an MMA fight, weight counts for a lot and the environment is totally different. MMA is a sport and not a real fight—you use different kinds of techniques because of the nature of the sport and concern for the safety for the fighters. It's about winning a trophy and not about self-defense.
Carlos "Caique" Elias

Professor Helio Gracie has proven that age is just a self-imposed limitation that can be exceeded. What a great example and what a courageous mind.
Helio "Soneca" Moreira

My father realized that the only way to prove jiu-jitsu was effective was to make vale tudo fights. That's the reason vale tudo was created. Once everybody in Brazil accepted what jiu-jitsu was about, it became unnecessary to keep challenging people. The point was proven.
Carlos Gracie Jr

I truly think that leg locks are part of grappling regardless of your style.
Eric Paulson

Strength is important but you can always get around it with good technique. So you have to be careful. Strength is a physical component that makes you explosive and for your adversaries, a harder opponent to deal with. But technique is more important because in the end is with a good technique that you finish the fight.
Frank Shamrock

Try to practice as much as you can because the more you train the better you'll be. The physical techniques have to be second nature.
Gene LeBell

As an instructor I make sure everything I teach works on the mat and the street. I don't teach things that can get my students hurt because they are useless and ineffective under real circumstances.
Gokor Chivichyan

Kimura was so impressed that he invited me to Japan to teach at his academy. But I kindly refused. I was very honored but I couldn't leave my family and go.
Helio Gracie

Martial arts, and especially jiu-jitsu, is like water: it fits in every shape and in every body.
Jean Jacques Machado

It is important to believe in yourself, but do it realistically and with common sense. You should know your limitations and work hard to at least reach those limits.

Helio "Soneca" Moreira

Royce Gracie is a classic jiu-jitsu man who gets his opponents down, tires them, and then submits them.

Marco Ruas

Today's fighters are the gladiators of the past. We are here to compete but they were there to save their lives. I believe we need to maintain that "gladiator mentality."

Mark Kerr

Nowadays martial arts are both sport and art but for most people they are mostly sport.

Matt Furey

To fight professionally you have to put yourself 100 percent into training and preparation. If your mind is someplace else it's difficult.

Oleg Taktarov

In order to win jiu-jitsu you have to study jiu-jitsu. It is that clear...in order to beat jiu-jitsu you have to analyze and study jiu-jitsu so in the very end, the victorious needs to know jiu-jitsu.

Relson Gracie

I have also incorporated some other aspects like takedowns and controls from wrestling into my game.
Renato Magno

If I feel I must do something and I might die, I don't care about my physical body. My spiritual body is more important.
Rickson Gracie

When you reach a certain level of effectiveness in jiu-jitsu, it changes your perspective. You start trusting yourself.
Rorion Gracie

I strongly believe that you have to be extremely fit to be ready for battle.
Royler Gracie

A fighter is not the one who knows only how to hit, but knows also how to be hit.
Wallid Ismael

There are some weak point in the human body that if you know how to manipulate and dig in with your knuckles and fingers, there's nothing the opponent can do.
Wally Jay

Sport jiu-jitsu is more of a friendly thing for relaxation. MMA is more extreme, with more possibilities. You have to be stronger mentally and physically.
Carlos Baretto

The most important thing is the fans. You can fight to win, but you had better fight for the fans, too. If you win the fight but lose the fans, you've lost everything. Better to lose the fight and win the fans.
Vitor Belfort

Competing gives you an edge that is impossible to have otherwise.
Wander Braga

I simply try to follow and maintain the Cahill tradition and the art my father John mastered under Henry Okazaki. I'm just doing my job and enjoying the process.
Willy Cahill

I only concentrate on today. Age is not a factor to me, the determining factor is my body.
Rickson Gracie

Once you transfer your knowledge and don't limit yourself by thinking that you're only a grappler or only a striker, you catch on. It's all in the head and how you think about yourself.
Rico Chiapparelli

Try to learn as much as possible and try to overlap all the information. It's not wise for a fighter to jump from style to style because he won't get too far. He should try to be a well-rounded fighter but stick to what he does best.
Randy Couture

People don't realize how hard it was to stand our ground in Rio against all the jiu-jitsu fighters. But I stood up for what I believed in, and it paid off in the end.
Hugo Duarte

We all have our own lives but it doesn't mean we have to negate our roots and recognized those who opened the doors for us.
Helio Gracie

The bottom line is that jiu-jitsu has to be natural. If there is any technique that is not natural, you will have a problem. That's why BJJ is so different from other arts.
Paulo Gillobel

Learn them all equally as you go, and don't get impatient. One day you will wake up, and you will be comfortable performing the techniques. Don't try to force your learning. It should be natural.
Carlson Gracie

Bigger and bigger guys were coming into the UFC and limiting the time really hurt me. I thought it created a huge disadvantage for me.
Royce Gracie

Rickson is a different fighter from anyone. He is a scientist of jiu-jitsu. His knowledge and skill is far and away above everybody else.
Fabio Gurgel

Learning a technique and mastering that technique are two different things. You can learn a key lock, but mastering it means you can do it even if your brains have been scrambled and fatigue has you on the verge of unconsciousness.
John Lewis

Teaching is a big part in my life and I hope I can keep doing for long time. It's a great sensation, a great feeling but it also bring a tremendous responsibility because people will follow what you tell them, so in many ways you are responsible for these people's growth.
Eric Paulson

Jiu-jitsu is great for kids because it teaches them respect and discipline and gives them something positive to do.
Cleber Luciano

If you think that you know everything after you get the black belt, you are wrong. This martial art is infinite.
Rodrigo Medeiros

Training for competition is a completely different thing than training for yourself and focusing on the true art of Brazilian jiu-jitsu.
Helio "Soneca" Moreira

If an instructor has sound motives and is well qualified, then it's more likely that the student will develop good quality.
Jason Morris

Martial artists who need to fight in the street degrade their technical ability and show their immaturity.
Nino Schembri

People know me now. I've been around forever. I took the sport of mixed martial arts into the mainstream ... or was always there with it.
Ken Shamrock

In training, you do not always face someone who you can control. Sooner or later you'll have to face someone who is better than you and who is capable of controlling you.
Mike Swain

Stick to the basics and train hard to make the basics work against any type of opponent and under any kind of situation. Don't waste time with new "technical fantasies" that will take you nowhere. Stick to the basics.
Helio Gracie

Motivation is something that you always need to work on, not only in jiu-jitsu, but even in life.
Leo Vieira

I personally don't believe in training six or seven hours per day; it's too much for your body.
Bas Rutten

When my father created vale tudo he was not making money. When my uncle Helio was fighting bigger and stronger opponents it was not for money. The reason they put themselves on the line was more important than money to them—it was prestige and recognition of their art.
Carlos Gracie Jr

It is very interesting to see how martial arts mentality has changed over the last fifteen years since the beginning of the UFC. Using the cross-training approach is something very common among the practitioners these days.
Eric Paulson

Strength is something that comes and goes depending of your training and age.
Frank Shamrock

In a real fight your techniques have to come out instinctively, and you have to repeat then in practice until they are recorded in your nervous system. It takes years for the physical techniques to become second nature but there's no other way.
Gene LeBell

Your personal training as an instructor is totally different from the goals you may have as a fighter. In some aspects, I dare say that they are opposites. What you need and want as a fighter is not necessarily what you need and want as an instructor.
Gokor Chivichyan

I firmly believe in helping people. That's why I departed from tradition, because I wanted to find better and easier ways of doing the things.
Helio Gracie

It doesn't matter how big or small you are, or what kind of physical problems that you have. You're just going to have to adjust the jiu-jitsu to you, not adjust yourself to the jiu-jitsu.
Jean Jacques Machado

Royce Gracie opened very big doors for other Brazilian fighters, including myself. His victories helped Brazilian martial artists to be respected and allowed us to show the world our techniques.
Marco Ruas

The saddest sight in the martial arts are the people who are so completely sold on their art that they are deaf, dumb and blind for the rest of their lives. No one art contains all the answers.
Matt Furey

Mixed martial arts and NHB are new styles; and styles to me are like religions. There is always someone waiting around the block to make money with a new style.
Oleg Taktarov

These days, everything happens very fast and you need to be explosive and powerful on the ground—much more than in the past, simply because good mat technique is not enough in competition.
Renato Magno

I can't be bought, and nobody can change my ideas. My philosophy is also to always support the people who stay with me. I never turn my back on a friend.
Rickson Gracie

It was a quest for genuine effectiveness that motivated my father to improve his fighting system and which has been the inspiration for the whole Gracie family.
Rorion Gracie

I believe in focusing mentally in order to truly achieve peak performance. The mental aspect is at least as important as the physical.
Royler Gracie

To become a champion you need a combination of physical ability, mental ability and spiritual ability.
Carlos Baretto

When I am in the U.S., I try to improve my skills in many different areas because there are a lot of good guys outside jiu-jitsu. So I train boxing, wrestling and whatever. I don't limit myself.
Vitor Belfort

Set goals according to each level of your training and practice consistently.
Wander Braga

The martial arts are a wide field. But the entire focal point of wrestling is combat, because we fight and compete every day. That's why the base and the sensitivity are so good. Everything is just shortened.
Rico Chiapparelli

Fighting is something violent, but we are athletes who practice a combat sport. We are there to test our skills, with regulations and sportsmanship.
Rickson Gracie

It is a constant internal challenge. Every time I step into the ring I feel I have to improve a little.
Randy Couture

Don't go in a dojo and start training without looking and comparing. You want to be a fighter, then go to train under a famous sensei who was a good fighter in his younger days. If you don't care about fighting and are more interested in budo, look for a dojo with good people and a real dedicated sensei even if he is not the greatest fighter.
Jon Bluming

A jiu-jitsu technique is not a ballet movement that all the dancers have to follow exactly. You have to understand the principles of why and how the technique works and then adapt it to your own body structure. Only then can you truly express real Brazilian jiu-jitsu.
Paulo Gillobel

People who know me know that I don't fight in weight divisions. Size doesn't matter to me. My opponents have mainly always been bigger than me.
Royce Gracie

Training under Rickson is a revealing experience, even if you're a world champion. With him I began to understand the "real" essence of jiu-jitsu principles.
Fabio Gurgel

When your body is in pain and you feel you cannot go on, a mastered technique could save the day. A technique that you have mastered will be available to you as easily as walking or breathing. Study hard and turn your techniques into natural reactions.
John Lewis

Competition goes away and disappears from your life when you reach a certain age, but the art stays with you forever if you are really interested in it.
Helio "Soneca" Moreira

What surprises me, it is that some members of the Gracie family and individuals that really know what it is, prefer to call it "Brazilian jiu-jitsu." Credit should be given where credit is due. If what I have developed is internationally known as Gracie jiu-jistu, that is what it should be called. There is no other way around it.
Helio Gracie

There are more wrestling and sambo-type moves in judo now.
Jason Morris

The person who practices jiu-jitsu or any other martial art needs to be humble enough to keep learning. Professor Helio Gracie is an example of a true martial artist.
Nino Schembri

There is a certain spiritual fulfillment that I get from doing the martial arts. I am not sure I can explain it, but it is very satisfying.
Mike Swain

Motivation usually is based on a reason to do something. If you have a strong reason to do a task, then the motivation is there.
Leo Vieira

If you are strictly a jiu-jitsu or wrestling competitor, adding punches and kicks to your arsenal won't do any good because you are not going to need it. On the contrary, if you are a MMA fighter then you need punching and kicking skills to complement your grappling skills.
Rickson Gracie

As far as weight training goes I only do biceps and triceps exercises. The rest of the time I use my own body weight to develop power—such as push-ups and squats. I use weights more when I want to gain some weight. Generally, I do it three times a week as part of my power training.
Bas Rutten

It's important to understand that the main self-defense methods are very dangerous. This is not only applies to jiu-jitsu but to other arts such as karate or kung-fu.
Carlos "Caique" Elias

Nowadays, vale tudo events around the world are just a good way for fighters to make money. It has became a show and a business—and the goal is different.
Carlos Gracie Jr

Things have changed and there is nothing wrong with learning and using what is truly useful and adapting that to your own personality and game.
Eric Paulson

I don't believe the theory that only technique is what you need. You need a certain amount of strength and sometimes strength can be the only way to escape from a difficult situation. So make sure you have it, just in case you need it.
Frank Shamrock

I don't do any weight training but I am not against it. If it is done the right way, I am all for it. Just remember that a martial artist should not train as a bodybuilder and it should not replace his martial arts training.
Gene LeBell

An important point about fighting professionally is that you have to prepare for it and put all your time and dedication into it.
Gokor Chivichyan

I'm very proud of my sons. Rorion worked very hard in the United States to promote jiu-jitsu. Of course, Royce and Rickson also did a great job and they have great reputations as fighters and teachers.
Helio Gracie

I think one must be a complete fighter and know how to punch, kick, and fight on the ground. If one just know one of these skills, forget it!
Marco Ruas

Success is a journey, not a destination. Once you stop learning, or think you know it all, you're through.
Matt Furey

You have to find what it is good for you and try to make it work, but there is not the ultimate style, because regulations direct the sport and the techniques and how they're used.
Oleg Taktarov

In some ways, you can't really compare what we have now with what we had in the early days.
Renato Magno

I have a philosophy of life that compensates my age, not by the fact of being afraid of getting old, but because I think that people have to live the moment intensely.
Rickson Gracie

When I arrived in America in the late '70s, I began teaching in my garage and decided to call it Gracie jiu-jitsu to differentiate from the Japanese jiu-jitsu some people here had heard about.
Rorion Gracie

The spirituality is an important factor, because it allows you to see things objectively and to recognize that your opponent is not your enemy.
Carlos Baretto

*If everybody does a little bit to help and to bring the sport up,
the sport of MMA is going to be the biggest thing in the world.*
Vitor Belfort

*Beginners should learn the basics because they need to establish a solid
foundation for the more advanced techniques. It is true, though, that
many people get bored and discouraged so they start focusing more on
different movements instead of working on the basics.*
Wander Braga

*The effectiveness of the jiu-jitsu developed by my family is proven.
Everybody knows and accepts that fact.*
Carlos Gracie Jr

*The biggest problem with people who don't know about fighting
is that they think a tough guy has to look a certain way or act a
certain way or be a certain way. They are drawn to the violent
visual aspects of it.*
Rico Chiapparelli

*I'm always training. So, when I have to prepare for a fight, I push a
little bit more and re-arrange my training sessions to specifically fit
what I need for that particular fight.*
Randy Couture

*I think BJJ is a way of life, a challenge, a physical chess game. It is
far more than simply fighting or grappling with another person.*
Paulo Gillobel

*If you goal is to be
a complete fighter,
well-rounded competitor
in Mixed Martial Arts
or NHB then you
need to approach you
training with a very
open mind. You need
to have kickboxing skill
and grappling elements
that you can combine
in a complete package.*
Eric Paulson

*You don't want to
suddenly change the
strategy that got you there and won a championship for you. When
I won the first UFC with the gi, I just naturally left it on and kept
going with it.*
Royce Gracie

*There are a lot of intricacies that happen during a fight that can totally
mess up a technique that you have been taught. A teacher with real
experience will be able to address those kinds of things while you are
learning.*
John Lewis

Teaching jiu-jitsu is a privilege that many people do not have.
Rodrigo Medeiros

My advice for those who are not interested in competition is to focus on developing great basics. Don't try to learn 20 different ways of passing the guard. Learn three or four basic techniques that encompass all the fundamental principles of passing your opponent's guard and work hard until you have mastered them.
Helio "Soneca" Moreira

The popularity the art has today, it is due to my son Rorion. He is the person who really made the name of Gracie jiu-jitsu well-known around the world. Very few people knew my jiu-jitsu and my name before Rorion came to America and created the UFC.
Helio Gracie

Judo is a consistent and established art by itself and doesn't need to add more and more techniques. However, there are certain technical elements found in other grappling methods that can be useful for a judo competitor.
Jason Morris

One of the most important things a man can do is create or write something that people are still talking about 200 years later.
Nino Schembri

Striving to be the best at whatever I do—at work or on the mat—is what keeps me motivated.
Mike Swain

In jiu-jitsu, my motivation is in the joy of training and competing, challenging myself every time I step into a mat.
Leo Vieira

When you go from gi to no gi, you need to know how to change and adapt your guard, your controls, your clinch, etc., otherwise you are going to be defeated.
Rickson Gracie

I try to build or create situations in my training so they are as clos e as possible to the competition.
Marcio Feitosa

My strength training is sport-specific. I don't push a weight above my shoulders in training because I don't do that in the ring. I want to do exercises that are going to strengthen my fighting skills.
Bas Rutten

For self-defense purposes you have to evaluate what is really happening in a street fight, and then choose the style or method that will deal with the circumstances. Jiu-jitsu is expressed in the way the techniques are executed, not in the effect these techniques have upon the opponent.
Carlos "Caique" Elias

Jiu-jitsu practitioners don't need to fight anymore to prove that Brazilian jiu-jitsu is an effective self-defense and fighting method. Everybody knows it is.
Carlos Gracie Jr

I did train and still train under Dan Inosanto. His teaching is always focused in showing and sharing experiences with the student so the student find his own personal way of expressing himself in martial arts.
Eric Paulson

I personally work with free weights to get the strength I need, but my routine changes often since I don't like to do the same program all the time.
Frank Shamrock

I like to teach at my dojo, up in the mountains. I only teach advanced students who have ability. I really like to learn new techniques from talented martial artists, but these techniques have to work under combative fighting.
Gene LeBell

I advocate for full contact in punches and kicks but I also understand that this is not suitable for everybody, so it is also good to have tournaments and championships that allow students to compete under more controlled sets of rules that prevents unnecessary injuries.
Gokor Chivichyan

If teach it the right way, Gracie Jiu-Jitsu can make you a better person and make you happier with yourself.
Helio Gracie

I do movements that a person with a normal left hand doesn't do, because that's the way that jiu-jitsu fits me. I have developed jiu-jitsu to fit my touch. And I don't see any other person who trains jiu-jitsu that does it with the same type of problem that I have.
Jean Jacques Machado

The fighter of the future will be a cross-training one—a complete fighter on the ground and standing up. Even jiu-jitsu fighters who started this kind of competition, are practicing stand-up today.
Marco Ruas

Strength and conditioning are the cornerstones of a good fighter. Then, your martial art technique.
Mark Kerr

I am always thirsty and hungry to learn more. It's like I'm in this river that I never leave. I'm always swimming in it and don't feel comfortable if I'm not in the water.
Matt Furey

Students need to reach a technical level in which they can control the timing of their breathing in relationship to their physical movements.
Helio "Soneca" Moreira

If you allow pants you'll see more leg locks, because it is then easier to grab the legs. If you allow a gi there will be less striking techniques because it is more difficult to punch when someone is grabbing your gi. The regulations determine the direction of the techniques and the evolution of the styles.
Oleg Taktarov

Don't get caught in the idea that because your body looks good after all the weight training and running that you are good at jiu-jitsu.
Renato Magno

With time, you can lose resistance but gain experience, so you gain energy.
Rickson Gracie

Courage is the cornerstone of the martial artist's character.
Shizuya Sato

I loved and admired my Uncle Carlos. He was the man who managed Helio's career and was the spiritual leader of the family, leaving us the priceless legacy of his life's work—his knowledge in the field of nutrition.
Rorion Gracie

I am very lucky to have a very understanding and supportive wife who has made my life easier rather than make it harder.
Royler Gracie

We are the real gladiators of the modern world. We have to let people know that this sport exists.
Vitor Belfort

Once you have a good and strong technical arsenal and game plan, all what you need is to be able of apply all the basic at will. That's what your dedication and training should be focused on, and not trying to create new things that are simply a reflection of your lack of skill in jiu-jitsu basics.
Helio Gracie

In Japan, the symbol of jiu-jitsu is water, because water is adaptable to any space. It is unbreakable, and it flows. Yet, it is always water. It changes its shape but not its form.
Paulo Gillobel

If you've done any combat form, any martial art, the actual combat part is meaningless, because the point is that you're supposed to do it to learn about yourself.
Rico Chiapparelli

One thing I never do is to think about my opponent as an individual. I don't get personal with him. I simply look at what he does. This allows me to better focus on the fighting aspects without getting involved in any personal facet of my opponent.
Randy Couture

The main difference between a fighter and a teacher is that a fighter does it for himself and a teacher is able to change people's lives through his teachings.
Rickson Gracie

It is important for a student to know what he is looking for and determine his priorities.
Wander Braga

In the original format of the UFC you never knew who you were going to face in the next round so you couldn't just train for one person like you can now. From a purely technical and physical perspective, it was much more challenging.
Royce Gracie

If history teaches us something, it is that human beings never learn from their mistakes.
Fabio Gurgel

There is no way to attain mastery of any martial art without using the mind.
Hayward Nishioka

The martial arts are like dancing. You have 100 percent control of your body and mind, and you are able to command it to move, bend and flow with no hesitation at any given moment. It is my ultimate form of expression. It is who I am.
John Lewis

For me, jiu-jitsu is a way of life, and it changed me.
Rodrigo Medeiros

Rice is rice but Brazilians and Chinese don't cook it the same! Jiu-jitsu is jiu-jitsu, but it should accommodate the culture of the country where the instructor teaches.
Helio "Soneca" Moreira

I live in the present so as long as I can feel my body working in the way it is now, I won't retire from fighting.
Rickson Gracie

Judo is the ultimate athletic activity to create coordination, strength, speed and self-confidence. It's a perfect athletic base for any sport.
Jason Morris

Jiu-jitsu is not something that you can leave at the academy. You need to take it home with you, feel it and then go back to the school to make it grow inside of you.
Nino Schembri

Judo is a sport under certain regulations for the competitor's safety. A self-defense situation is everything but safe.
Mike Swain

I don't look for fights. I don't need to brawl in the streets to prove that I can fight. I don't need it, and I don't think it brings a good reputation to the art of jiu-jitsu either.
Leo Vieira

Sometimes I gain a lot of strength and muscle mass very quickly, so I have to cut back my training. I don't feel comfortable carrying around too much weight—it slows me down.
Bas Rutten

I have seen a lot of people mixing different styles of martial arts—but that is very difficult. It is one thing to take elements from other methods to make what you are already doing better, and it is another thing to mix styles thinking that you are going to become better.
Carlos "Caique" Elias

The beginning students should be patient and hang in there until they get good results, otherwise they will not succeed in jiu-jitsu.
Carlos Gracie Jr

I'm a professional fighter. Of course, that I use part of the elements from Jun Fan/Jeet Kune Do but mainly tactics and fighting strategies. My techniques are a combination of several fighting arts and combat sports. As a "ring" fighter I need to look for different things.
Eric Paulson

If you lift heavy weights and don't stretch you are going to have some problems, because you'll get tight and slow.
Frank Shamrock

I always looked for the best teacher in the particular aspects I wanted to develop. No teacher can give you everything you need so don't be afraid and look for the one who can provide you with the things you want.
Jon Bluming

When I fought I did it for a cause and for a reason. The reason was to prove the efficiency of the method of jiu-jitsu that I was developing. I never did for money. Today, fighters do it simply for money, that's their only objective and goal.
Helio Gracie

As you mature and grow you realize that fighting has a lot of mental aspects that you didn't know about when you were younger.
Marco Ruas

Nowadays, fighters are all very well-rounded and they know how to punch, kick, and fight on the ground, so taking advantage of the other fighter's weakness is more a matter of training for what the fighter specifically does, rather than a particular set of techniques.
Gokor Chivichyan

Practice religiously and devote yourself to the task. Learn to use your mind and to develop your mind.
Matt Furey

MMA and NHB methods are combat or fighting sports, not a pure self-defense methods.
Oleg Taktarov

In sport jiu-jitsu, the techniques change and evolve all the time— a competitor needs to be updated constantly. A regular student who trains jiu-jitsu for self-defense and for fun doesn't need to worry about all that.
Renato Magno

Fear is always present. For me that's good. You must be afraid. If you're not afraid, you're not intelligent.
Rickson Gracie

The credit for the refinement of the traditional Japanese system, which gave birth to what is known today as Gracie or Brazilian jiu-jitsu goes to the one-and-only Helio Gracie.
Rorion Gracie

I'm just a guy who wants to live simply, enjoy life and prove I can do good.
Vitor Belfort

Jiu-jitsu is a great exercise and you'll be spending a lot of time at the school. You want to make sure that the people at the school are the kind of individuals who will bring positive things into your life.
Wander Braga

I want my students to be able of reaching a high level of skill in the shortest possible time and in order to achieve that we have to use proven scientific training methods.
Eric Paulson

Rickson Gracie is the only person making real money in NHB. He has a knowledge of marketing and the ability to hold himself back.
Rico Chiapparelli

Stretching relaxes my body and allows me to recover from strenuous training sessions. I do my flexibility exercises before and after every training practice.
Randy Couture

That is how I see jiu-jitsu and that's how the art should be used in competition. I also think it is how we should act in our personal lives.
Paulo Gillobel

The food you take is the fuel of your body. Your body will perform according to the type of food you put in it.
Frank Shamrock

Strategy is always a matter of different factors. Even when you don't know who you're fighting or what they like to do, you will find out quickly when you press an attack.
Royce Gracie

It is easy to talk about what you could do, but quite another thing to put it all on the line and step into that cage in front of everyone.
John Lewis

Jiu-jitsu calmed me down mentally and gave me a much more cooperative attitude towards my family and people in general.
Cleber Luciano

You have to determine your strong points and emphasize those.
Rodrigo Medeiros

A technical jiu-jitsu practitioner, even if he is a high belt, can train with lower belts and get a great workout.
Helio "Soneca" Moreira

Fighting without a gi cuts the number of possibilities down so the basics can be mastered in a shorter period of time.
Rickson Gracie

Train with sincerity and the right spirit. Consistency will bring results, and don't forget that you learn judo by doing judo.
Jason Morris

We all need to find those things that bring us peace and tranquility. Only then can we face the challenges of daily life. It is that way with martial arts.
Nino Schembri

You must know how to fight and how to take care of yourself in the dojo and in the street.
Jon Bluming

A real self-defense situation has almost nothing to do with a tournament. The street is a completely different environment that brings many other elements into the equation.
Mike Swain

Jiu-jitsu is an art based on using leverage, not brute force.
Leo Vieira

Once you build that habit, the gi, the dojo, your instructor and your teammates will be a continuation of your body and your mind.
Marcio Feitosa

Regardless of your chosen direction in the arts, discipline and hard training is what it will bring back to you a feeling of joy. You need to put yourself 100% in your training. If you are a fighter even more than 100%. In life you get back what you put in and martial arts is not an exception.
Eric Paulson

Diet and nutrition are very important aspects of a fighter. I believe in consistency so I don't change eating habits as I get close to a fight. This means that I always have to control what I eat. I have a real tendency to eat junk food!
Bas Rutten

Martial Arts are a way of life. It doesn't mean a thing if someone performs a technique much better than another student, it's the pureness of that person's heart that counts.
Shizuya Sato

My opinion is that mixing styles confuses the student and puts them in a very difficult situation if they face a real self-defense situation.
Carlos "Caique" Elias

If you quit early in your training, you are apt to be discouraged and developed a negative attitude towards yourself. Throughout your life, the tendency to give up prematurely will stifle the development of the self-confidence which comes from accomplishment.
Carlos Gracie Jr

I'm a very focused person and I know what I want and what it works in the ring. Professional fighters know and this is something that I want to pass to my students; that knowledge of what it works and why it does.
Eric Paulson

Stretching and flexibility are essential for me. The more you work out, the more you train, more stiff you get. With age you don't get more flexible but more rusty.
Frank Shamrock

Be ready for everything. Don't challenge people. Make friends and then be there when they need you. Don't keep secrets. Teach what you know because that's what people appreciate the most—honesty.
Gene LeBell

There is so much knowledge out there to be absorbed, and I enjoy the idea of training with all good teachers of martial arts. But don't get me wrong, I'm not only talking about the techniques, a good teacher teaches you the right attitude and spirit as well.
Gokor Chivichyan

Fighters today are truly professionals, there is a whole industry that allows a lot of people make a lot of money fighting in MMA. As far as that is concerned we cannot compare my times with the current ones.
Helio Gracie

You really have to believe in yourself. And I think that if you really believe in yourself, you can do anything you want. No doubt about it.
Jean Jacques Machado

Swimming is a very important part of my training program. It's a great cardiovascular workout and relaxes the muscles and doesn't put any stress in your joints.
Marco Ruas

I always considered intelligence to be one of the fighter's more important tools. In order to be a winner you need to have a game plan and you need to know your opponent.
Mark Kerr

I follow a system of deep breathing exercises that simultaneously energize my body and rid it of anything stressful that may interfere with me giving my all.
Matt Furey

Self-defense is a completely different ball game. Self-defense is not a sport, it is simply survival.
Oleg Taktarov

As martial artist we should look for quality and if someone is better in a certain fighting aspect there is nothing wrong with going to learn from that person.
Relson Gracie

The principles and concept s of Brazilian jiu-jitsu cannot be changed. They are the same for everybody and standard throughout the world and every student learns them.
Renato Magno

It's very important that you respect your opponent and be afraid of what he can do. But this goes back to emotional control. Don't let the fear get strong. It's there, but you keep it in a shell.
Rickson Gracie

Don't let the fact that you have or don't have a gi throw you off your grappling strategy—don't let it take you out of your game. Control the situation rather than letting the situation control you.
Rigan Machado

Let's face it, Helio Gracie is the embodiment of jiu-jitsu!
Rorion Gracie

Submission grappling is a much more slippery fight than BJJ, because of the fact you don't wear a gi, and the need is for quick explosive motion rather than slow and methodical techniques.
Royler Gracie

I look at small circle ju-jitsu as something very revolutionary, not just evolutionary. The whole world is changing so we have to evolve and improve in order to keep up with the new things.
Wally Jay

You don't need to be rich or famous to live well. Sometimes the rich live worse than the poor. If you're rich inside with family and friends, it doesn't matter how much money you have.
Vitor Belfort

The important things are family, good friends, and health. Put the rest aside. Good people bring good energy. And good energy brings success.
Wander Braga

Everyone should take a lesson from Rickson Gracie on how to market himself, how to get your price, how to keep adding to your reputation.
Rico Chiapparelli

Cardio is the very basis of every athlete. No cardiovascular resistance and you are done in fighting. I consider this to be the most important part of any athlete's training program.
Randy Couture

You need to respect the fighters above you because you are going to have to learn from them. You have to respect everyone but fear no one.
Paulo Gillobel

As a teacher you must be connected to the overall philosophy of incorporating martial arts into your life and not necessarily with the fighting aspects or elements of competition.
Rickson Gracie

In my dojo there are no religious talk, no discriminations on any kind of race, color, et cetera. No Bs, just training.
Jon Bluming

Royce Gracie's victories were good for everyone, and he is probably the single reason you see jiu-jitsu everywhere. Because of Royce, everyone knows about jiu-jitsu now. He did everyone a great service, and he deserves to be admired for what he did.

Carlson Gracie

Mental agility is probably more important than physical agility. The time on the mat sparring teaches your mind to work quickly, as well as your body.

Royce Gracie

We should work together and try to push the sport in a strong direction instead of weakening it by fighting and arguing among ourselves.

Fabio Gurgel

You have to have a little bit of fearlessness and a lot of heart to make it through the tough moments.

John Lewis

Jiu-jitsu for me is more than a martial art and more than my work; it is my hobby and my life!

Rodrigo Medeiros

The Ultimate Fighting Championship brought everyone's eyes to Brazilian jiu-jitsu and spread it all over the world.
Helio "Soneca" Moreira

My philosophy of life is to respect everybody and everything, trying to do my best in whatever I'm involved at that particular time.
Rickson Gracie

Preparation has been the key word in my life, not only in judo but in everything I do. The more prepared you are the better chance you give yourself to win.
Jason Morris

Championship performance comes only from the champion himself. A thousand perfect lessons cannot guarantee improvement.
Nino Schembri

I'm much better now than I ever was in the early UFCs. Obviously, back then I was younger and had more jump in my step, but my approach to a fight, my set-ups and my understanding of my opponent is far superior.
Ken Shamrock

In jiu-jitsu, "body feel" is the key. You have to develop specific physical attributes to make the techniques work.
Leo Vieira

Cardiovascular conditioning is the most important aspect in a fighter's routine. If your cardio is not good, it's like a car without gas—it's that simple. It doesn't matter if you have all the techniques in the world, if you don't have air then you're out of business.
Bas Rutten

Judo is a direct descendent of the traditional Japanese jiu-jitsu systems, so there are bound to be some similarities. Personally, I believe the changes that Jigoro Kano made to jiu-jitsu, when he turned it into judo, left judo with only a surface similarity to the original art.
Carlos "Caique" Elias

Anyone who undertakes jiu-jitsu training must be determined to stay, otherwise they will lose something very important—the opportunity to know themselves, their potential, and their personal abilities.
Carlos Gracie Jr

The JKD mentality passed to me by Dan Inosanto is what made me be open mined about incorporating techniques and moves from Wrestling to Brazilian jiu-jitsu, and from jiu-jitsu to sambo, and from savate to Thai boxing, et cetera. I don't see any problem or any boundaries as long as they create and fit into a compact and cohesive fighting structure that can be used in a fight against a skilled opponent.
Eric Paulson

I look at my stretching time as a moment to relax and feel in touch with my inner-self. I relax and breathe properly so I can stretch those muscles naturally without bouncing up and down.
Frank Shamrock

Don't forget that in order to get better you need to enjoy what you are doing. If you don't like the style you're practicing, you won't go very far—you'll get bored, tired, and your motivation will fly out the window.
Gokor Chivichyan

I can't compensate my lack of technique with strength because I don't have it. I have to make sure I do the technique 100 percent perfect.
Helio Gracie

People know the link of our family with the Gracie family and that means quality in the art. Our jiu-jitsu came from the Gracie family, and we are happy to admit that & we're proud of it.
Jean Jacques Machado

In MMA you need a certain amount of body weight and muscle mass to be successful.
Marco Ruas

If I see a teacher who has great body awareness and movement, I'm going to study him and see how I can fit it into what I do.
Matt Furey

The best kicking techniques for fighting are the Thai boxing kicks. Keep them low and to the point!
Oleg Taktarov

The importance is about how to master the basics and not in learning a lot of competition techniques. It's in separate classes for those who want to compete, where you can focus on technical aspects more suitable for sport.
Renato Magno

Our jiu-jitsu is something you can do for your entire lifetime. My father ensured that our philosophy and techniques would work whether you are big and very strong or small and frail. It is all about leverage and feel.
Rickson Gracie

I just want to be a good fighter, a good person, and to be respected by people.
Rigan Machado

Orientals bow to each other as a cultural habit. I don't teach Oriental culture, I teach Gracie jiu-jitsu, and a simple handshake is good enough.
Rorion Gracie

In grappling without a gi, you need to be very active and be constantly on the move—so I train for this by constantly shifting positions with my training partners.
Royler Gracie

A strong spirit is necessary to choose the right way and not the bad. I only believe in my success if I'm still training hard.
Wallid Ismael

Within the context of the fighting sports, nobody is better than anyone else. Each person is trained and wants to win.
Carlos Baretto

If you don't have the passion to share and spend time taking care of people, then teaching is not for you. It's that simple.
Rickson Gracie

I want to help people in ways that money cannot buy. Maybe by seeing what I do they can see that they can also achieve their goals.
Vitor Belfort

Relaxation is very important before a match, so I will visualize how things might happen and go through different scenarios. This makes me feel more confident and prepared.
Wander Braga

It's easy to sit back and talk about anyone. But who knows what's going on in their personal lives, in their heads and in the life that they lead and with the people they're surrounded with.
Rico Chiapparelli

It's important that every aspect of the training has a purpose and perfectly overlaps with the rest to achieve the desired result.
Randy Couture

If you want to be a BJJ competitor, you have to spend all your time on the mat training. Judo and wrestling will help in this.
Paulo Gillobel

I like to train against really big and strong guys, because most of the people I fought were bigger than me. So I wanted to feel weight, strength and power during my preparation.
Royce Gracie

In our days, in any sport you need the weight training to supplement your skills but in a scientific way under the guidance of a real teacher who knows what he is doing in your particular discipline. It is call specific training.
Jon Bluming

In the old days, we used to fight for the simple pleasure of defending our art and to be recognized as a fighter. Fighting for your style was the main reason for vale tudo fights.
Fabio Gurgel

You have to be able to take your falls like a man and your wins like a champion.
John Lewis

If you want to seriously improve your game, you need to find the right sparring partners.
Helio "Soneca" Moreira

All sports teach many of the tools necessary for success in life if you know how to look under the surface.
Jason Morris

Winning is not found by whom you learn from in the academy but rather in the heart of the fighter who brings dedication and intelligence to a realistic and complete program.
Nino Schembri

*Good conditioning,
good technique and—
most importantly—
an awesome fighting
spirit. I think these
three characteristics
sum it all up.*
Mike Swain

*Find a training
partner who helps
you train and
improve your
technique, not
a brainless tough
guy who is going
to hurt you.*
Leo Vieira

*Jiu-jitsu has made me a person angry for learning and jiu-jitsu
has taught me that the most important thing is that there is always
something you don't know.*
Marcio Feitosa

*As teacher you have to give the student everything you have: your
experience, your knowledge and you time. You can't give him your
talent or your feeling for the art. You do your half and the rest
is on the student's shoulders.*
Rickson Gracie

What I do the most of the time is combine grappling with a partner for two minutes and then kick the bag for one minute. Then I repeat this routine for eight rounds. My partner rests as I kick the bag, so when I go back he's fresh and I am more tired. It takes a lot out of me.
Bas Rutten

I see champions who are able to display a great amount of technique, but who lack high technical skill and understanding of the basics.
Carlos Gracie Jr

Regardless of how many years of training you have, you need to have that mentality to expose yourself in someone else's art (class) and learn, and at the same time place yourself in a vulnerable position to learn more, with the same passion and desire of a white belt (beginner).
Eric Paulson

Breathing is vital in all kind of elasticity and flexibility programs. This is one of the most important components in a professional fighter. All the great fighters, regardless of sport, are extremely flexible.
Frank Shamrock

I believe that your own spirituality as an individual has a lot to do with the motivation you need to gain success in life.
Marco Ruas

When you look in the mirror each day, if the person staring back is half-ass at everything he does, then how can he radiate confidence?
Matt Furey

I truly love the martial arts, so for me to keep training and teaching does not require a big effort. I'm blessed because I am doing what I love, so I consider myself a lucky person.
Gokor Chivichyan

My strategy never was to remain on the bottom and tire my opponent. That's something that I had to do for obvious reasons. It was a consequence, not my way of fighting. I have always fought bigger and stronger opponents, some of them simply grabbed my gi and put me on the ground.
Helio Gracie

Some people don't like the idea of weight training but believe me, it is necessary these days. Skill by itself is not enough.
Oleg Taktarov

"Brazilian jiu-jitsu" is the term used to describe a certain style of jiu-jitsu that is not Japanese—and I think this is good because not all the jiu-jitsu styles are the same.
Carlos "Caique" Elias

It's important to be humble and acknowledge that there are areas where you can improve.
Relson Gracie

Never let the weights rule your technique but use that extra strength to sharpen your skills and keep your speed and mobility as a middleweight.
Jon Bluming

An instructor needs to control and regulate the classes so the students know how much pressure to apply without hurting each other.
Renato Magno

In my jiu-jitsu you can still defeat most opponents quickly with little effort, no matter how you are feeling at that most important moment.
Rickson Gracie

I saw in the UFC an opportunity to expose to the world the truths and fallacies inherent in contemporary martial arts theory.
Rorion Gracie

One needs to have a strong spirit not to be taken by the extremes: at the top not to let it go to your head and at the bottom not to let it defeat you.
Wallid Ismael

I know that people, after training in martial arts, don't have to prove themselves anymore. They become better human beings.
Wally Jay

I never think I have an advantage when I fight anyone. It's important to stay humble and focused. I just think about getting ready and not getting too confident.
Vitor Belfort

To have confidence in your technique, you need to have proper training in the fundamentals so they become automatic reflexes. Only then can you be relaxed in a fight.
Wander Braga

Who am I to criticize anyone, and say they're right or wrong? I can comment or observe, but that's it. You can't judge anyone else because you don't live his life.
Rico Chiapparelli

It's my responsibility now to transmit my experiences and knowledge to my students in the proper way.
Rickson Gracie

Every fighter has a strong point that he capitalizes on when he fights. The key is to find what this strong point is and nullify it so he can't rely on it. When it's neutralized, it decreases his confidence.
Randy Couture

If you want to be a MMA fighter, you have to study a martial art that teaches you how to strike and to defend against punches and kicks. This kind of training will give you more options when you are facing an opponent in the cage.
Paulo Gillobel

The biggest joy and my most important moment was my win over Waldemar Santana. The Gracie name was low at the time, and I was able to bring it to the top again.
Carlson Gracie

Any free time I have I want to spend with them. I don't want to be just a fictitious father; I want to be there for them. I want to teach them about life, and I want to teach them how to become adults.
Royce Gracie

Now all fighters know a little of everything, and the best man wins, independent of his fighting style. A true mixed-martial-arts style has been developed due to the UFC and other similar events.
Fabio Gurgel

Invincibility begins and exists within an unbeatable mind. If your mind doesn't believe that you are invincible, you remain beatable because your mind accepts the possibility of defeat.
John Lewis

Jiu-jitsu teaches fighting techniques to kids but it also teaches kids not to fight. It will change your attitude for the better.
Cleber Luciano

Combat jiu-jitsu is a martial art that can't be trained unless you hurt your partner, but sport jiu-jitsu allows practitioners to test their skills safely.
Helio "Soneca" Moreira

It is important to put time and energy into training sessions because they are the trigger factors for your mental state.
Jason Morris

You need to supplement and support your pure jiu-jitsu training with any other aspects that will make you better and stronger.
Nino Schembri

The key to making jiu-jitsu techniques work is leverage, but strength is also necessary. Don't think that technique will work by itself because it will not.
Leo Vieira

When I teach, for me it's something very special. I do it with love. I'm sharing an art created by my family so in a way I'm sharing one of my family assets.
Rickson Gracie

As far as flexibility goes, I stretch the whole body. When you are young you don't need it as much as when you get older!
Bas Rutten

Martial arts are a great way of life. They give me a peace of mind that helps to balance the rest of my life.
Gokor Chivichyan

In the basic techniques, you have the necessary tools that will open doors for a more evolved technical game. But if you spend less and less time on the basics because you need to catch up on all the new modifications, you'll end up with many weak positions and few strong one.
Carlos Gracie Jr

I always felt fear. It's a natural thing and a human sensation. If you say you don't feel fear I think you are lying. It's not a fear that won't allow you to move a finger but it's that sensation about the unknown what keeps you wondering and keeps you going.
Eric Paulson

If you are in better shape than your opponent, you can outlast the guy. If you are not in shape, then the game is over. You can't win.
Frank Shamrock

I don't believe that a teacher should hold back techniques. Why take secrets to your grave? When you die you live on through your students.
Gene LeBell

There is nothing wrong with the sport aspect of jiu-jitsu; just keep in mind that it is only a sport and not a real self-defense situation.
Carlos "Caique" Elias

When you are on the ground the bigger opponent always will use the bodyweight advantage to stay on the top. It's a natural thing but remain on the bottom was never my strategy, it was the result of circumstances and never my goal. I couldn't choose.
Helio Gracie

It is very important to understand that today being good in jiu-jitsu is not enough anymore. Years ago if a bigger and stronger guy didn't know jiu-jitsu it was easy to defeat him. Today the big and strong guys know jiu-jitsu so if you are not in top physical conditioning you are going to be in hot water!
Jean Jacques Machado

Stay humble and not become a nuisance once you become a champion. For not following these important rules I kicked out of my dojo in 1964 the most famous judoka whoever came from the Western world: the twice Olympic medal winner and three times world champion, Willem Ruska.
Jon Bluming

I always set goals and then work to accomplish them. Every goal is a project that I have to finish. I take one step at a time and pace myself properly to reach the finish line.
Marco Ruas

We all have our fears. The trick is knowing how to canalize this fear and make it work for you. Fear is good, it makes you be aware of things and not to think you're too good!
Mark Kerr

Any desire you have, so long as you can picture it in your mind and back it up with a burning desire, you can manufacture that result in reality.
Matt Furey

I like to train in a relaxed atmosphere so my motions become reflex, natural reactions, instinctive responses. This is the only way you can become one with your art, making your training melt with your human essence and inner self.
Relson Gracie

Keeping a student in a belt rank too long is as unfair as giving out a belt too fast. In the very end, it boils down to the instructor's honesty.
Renato Magno

My family has fought in the dojo, in the ring, in the streets and on the beaches of Brazil. We are always training and always ready for the challenge.
Rickson Gracie

You have to be well-rounded in order to win. It's a combination of things that makes a fighter a champion these days.
Oleg Taktarov

When you impose a time limit, you are in effect giving a fighter a psychological "safety net."
Rorion Gracie

You can train all you want and spend hours sparring in your studio, but you don't know what you have inside until you step onto the mat or into the ring in a real competition or fight.
Carlos Baretto

Don't give up when things get tough and remember that there are many different ways of achieving what you want.
Wander Braga

The martial arts are a process and all practitioners should enjoy them without adding unnecessary pressure. Live your life truly and honestly.
Willy Cahill

Competition is something good, especially when you are young.
Rickson Gracie

Every action has an effect on every thought and every thought affects every action.
Shizuya Sato

It's a whole different thing when you go out there and they shut the cage and you're in there. It makes you learn more about yourself and why you are who you are—it's a defining moment.
Rico Chiapparelli

Without confidence a fighter is nothing. If a fighter doesn't believe in himself, in what he has, in the hard training he went through, then it is better he doesn't step into the Octagon.
Randy Couture

You can use fear to your own advantage because you need fear to develop courage. A good fighter overcomes his fear.
Paulo Gillobel

To fight MMA, everybody has to cross-train. That's a plain fact. There is no other way now.
Royce Gracie

Training for a fight should initially entail four to five hours of intense training focusing heavily on conditioning and endurance.
John Lewis

Jiu-jitsu is natural, so you shouldn't do anything artificial.
Rodrigo Medeiros

To be honest, I don't have a special mental and philosophical preparation for a competition. I know that whatever I may accomplish is coming from God, so I simply consider myself a vehicle.
Helio "Soneca" Moreira

Character is what makes an individual; it is what sets him apart from the rest of the crowd.
Jason Morris

When someone starts to feel too much fear in training or competition, that means he is not controlling himself mentally.
Nino Schembri

Technique is what you actually use in competition, but all the other aspects of the physical conditioning are the elements that make the technique work under pressure.
Mike Swain

Training in jiu-jitsu for me is both a mental and physical therapy. It is an important part of my life. Honestly, I can't picture myself without jiu-jitsu being part of my life. But don't get me wrong ... life is bigger and more important than jiu-jitsu.
Leo Vieira

In the very beginning I basically learned grappling from watching tapes. When I decided to focus on grappling I got together with a good friend of mine, Leon Van Dyke. We used to work out twice a day in grappling. It was during these sparring sessions that we found a lot of useful movements and techniques.
Bas Rutten

If you only train a little bit for self-defense then there are hundreds of movements that you don't need to know—basically because you only need a very direct and simple approach for self-protection. But if you are training and competing in sport jiu-jitsu, that's another story.
Carlos "Caique" Elias

My advice to students is to spend more time on the basic techniques instead of diversifying your training into an endless number of techniques that will bring you momentary recognition.
Carlos Gracie Jr

What is important is how a fighter deal with the sensation of fear, how he faces those feelings and makes them work positively for him. There is a psychological process behind this and that's the reason why professional boxers have psychologists in their training camps.
Eric Paulson

For me, conditioning is the most important thing you can do to your body. Knowing that you are a conditioned fighter will build confidence in your mind because you know you can perform the actions and pull the techniques off.
Frank Shamrock

Competition is a sport and not a real fight.
Gokor Chivichyan

If you are not fully capable of using the guard, then it doesn't take a great fighter to pass the guard, but this doesn't mean the guard is not good anymore or you shouldn't use it because people now know how to pass it.
Helio Gracie

Martial arts have become combat sports. And MMA is a complete fighting sport.
Mark Kerr

Practice is an opportunity to know the self. When I practice, I am as much aware as what I am thinking as what I am doing. I stay conscious and live in the moment.
Matt Furey

You put yourself into a mental state that allows you to step into the ring and fight. Everything around you becomes a silent movie, you see but you don't hear.
Oleg Taktarov

Being a good fighter or competitor does not necessarily mean you'll be a good teacher.
Renato Magno

Yes, everyone can be beaten, and I know this. But as of yet, I have not been.
Rickson Gracie

The effectiveness of our system is due to its simplicity—and it's far better to learn them one-on-one where we can coach the student individually instead of telling a whole class to play follow the leader and hope they can keep up.
Rorion Gracie

The important thing to keep in mind is that you need to do your homework and find something that works for you and then keep improving it.
Royler Gracie

It's important to train hard, be healthy and do the right things.
Vitor Belfort

*Being humble means having an
open attitude to learn and gain
knowledge and to endure sweat
and pain while trying to improve
your skills. It means thinking
that you are still a beginner
and still have a lot to learn.*
Wander Braga

*In the cage, there is no place
to hide and no one to pass
the blame to. It's just you,
your opponent and a
chain-link fence.*
Rico Chiapparelli

*A winning attitude is everything. A fighter needs a positive frame of
mind to successfully confront his opponent.*
Randy Couture

*If something scares you, you should face it. If you do that, you have
beaten fear. Courage is nothing more than having done something
before.*
Paulo Gillobel

*I am all for sports jiu-jitsu, but we need to remember why people started
to learn martial arts in the first place!*
Royce Gracie

If your mind is strong and free of all negative influence, the battle is 75 percent won. All that remains for this warrior is to achieve his optimal physical level of external conditioning and make sure that his weapons are sharp and ready for combat.
John Lewis

In 1995, I had a serious back injury. My doctor said I should start thinking about stopping jiu-jitsu completely. The back is an important part of your body if you train in jiu-jitsu. It is like having a shoulder injury in boxing; yes, you can use your hands, but you do not have the physical support system. That is what the back represents to a jiu-jitsu student. I had to re-evaluate my training, select the people I could train with and determine what kind of techniques I'd do.
Helio "Soneca" Moreira

Today, if you teach students the rigid, traditional way, you are going to lose 90 percent of them. You have to use a more modern approach now.
Jason Morris

As a teacher you influence your students' lives in many ways. The goal is different and more relevant.
Rickson Gracie

To reach the mental level required for successful competition, you have to learn to rely on your mind to defeat that weakening fear.
Nino Schembri

It is better to know fewer techniques that actually work than many techniques which are useless. Every move I make works—either in the ring or in the street.
Bas Rutten

Competition is what raises the level of any sport—be it basketball, jiu-jitsu, karate, or football. The need to get better and improve is what makes athletes look for new techniques and approaches.
Carlos "Caique" Elias

No basics, no nothing. It's that simple.
Carlos Gracie Jr

The mind is the most powerful tool but also the most dangerous. If five minutes before a fight your mind goes in the wrong direction and starts thinking the wrong things, chances are you'll end up losing the fight.
Eric Paulson

In martial arts you need to train your body to do specific activities, on command and reflexively. It's only by repetitive training that your body can do those fighting motions.
Frank Shamrock

Fighting in the street is a lose-lose situation. Even if you win, there is a big loss in who you are. A true martial artist should be above all these childish ego games.
Gokor Chivichyan

*If you don't know
how to properly use
the guard, people
are going to pass it,
but that's not the
guard's fault, it's
your fault. And
that's what is
happening today.*
Helio Gracie

*You have to be flexible enough to change your goals if circumstances
change. Life often takes different directions that you have no control
over, and your goals should adapt to your current situation and
environment.*
Marco Ruas

*Believe me, the more attention you pay to the external factors
surrounding a fight, the less focused you are the day of the fight.*
Oleg Taktarov

*The instructor grows by his student's success. The better your students
are, the better instructor and martial artist you will be.*
Relson Gracie

*A good teacher will always know how to help the students recognize
and deal with the important points of any technique.*
Renato Magno

The only guy I ever challenged was Mike Tyson because he said in a magazine that he's the best fighter in the word. And I don't believe that; being the best boxer in the world doesn't mean that individual is the best fighter.
Rickson Gracie

We don't want the students to memorize the moves. We teach their subconscious to react, which is faster than the conscious mind.
Rorion Gracie

Try to be in good shape all the time. Keep your body clean and follow a good nutritional plan. Food is the fuel of your body.
Wander Braga

We are all capable of doing what we want. All it takes is hard work, discipline, determination, desire and faith in God. Everything is possible.
Vitor Belfort

It is important to know how to control negative thoughts. It is critical to intercept them and keep them at bay. This is a very important ability that can be used in any field in life, not just fighting.
Randy Couture

Keep training and believe that you are learning the best martial art ever. BJJ is growing fast and one day, for sure, it will be a very big sport.
Paulo Gillobel

The UFC used to be style against style. Now it is fighter against fighter. It's man against man.
Royce Gracie

In reality, no one is truly invincible, but you must learn to approach each battle, each test in life with the outlook and intensity of the invincible warrior. The mystery of life is free choice.
John Lewis

I had to limit the weight of my sparring partners because heavier guys would seriously hurt my back. I also had to avoid training with people who used only brute force and pure strength.
Helio "Soneca" Moreira

Fear is a good thing and it partially is what drives athletes to train. When fear gets too strong, however, it can prevent an athlete from performing his best.
Jason Morris

Mental flexibility—keep your mind open to everything. Don't do something just because somebody says so. See if you can find out if it's good and then use it.
Bas Rutten

Brazilian jiu-jitsu practitioners are developing new techniques all the time, and if you are not aware of this then you won't be winning. It's that simple.
Carlos "Caique" Elias

Competition has affected the way many practitioners train jiu-jitsu, and the perception of the outside world is that jiu-jitsu is simply competition due to the way most instructors teach it.
Carlos Gracie Jr

Do your best in every training session, in every drill in every move, because when you give your 110% then you know that you are ready. Knowing that you are ready will automatically bring confidence within your mind and that's the key ingredient to overcome fear: confidence.
Eric Paulson

The cardiovascular training gives you that gas to reach the finishing line. You have the best submission technique when your body is in top condition. If you don't follow a good cardio program, you won't last very long in a fight.
Frank Shamrock

If you need to get into fights to prove anything, then you need to re-evaluate who you are and what you are doing in martial arts— because there is something wrong with you.
Gokor Chivichyan

The only way you can win a top jiu-jitsu fighter is with jiu-jitsu. The way I developed the jiu-jitsu techniques make the art almost an inexpugnable fortress.
Helio Gracie

Your mind and the thoughts you think are your supreme weapon.
Matt Furey

Martial arts gave me a new direction in life. I had other goals, but my training helped me to focus on the aspects that were important.
Oleg Taktarov

The essence of jiu-jitsu is to let the technique explode from within. You must use the art with feeling.
Renato Magno

It's impossible to know when you are "fully" prepared for a fight. That's something that you never know.
Rickson Gracie

It's a simple matter of developing strong basics—the kind of foundation that eventually allows the student to become really efficient.
Rorion Gracie

I truly believe that fights are won or lost outside of the limelight, way before you step into the arena.
Royler Gracie

In MMA, I believe that fighters should be treated much better than they are now. They should get paid bigger sums of money because they are the ones making everything possible.
Wander Braga

Focus on the positive and block the negative. This enables you to work in the right direction with the right mental attitude.
Randy Couture

If you let fear take control of you, it is going to be hard to succeed in a fight or in life.
Paulo Gillobel

I have learned that you can't change people that much from how they naturally are. You can't turn a leopard into a lion.
Royce Gracie

When you bring something new to wrestling, they get defensive and it upsets them. It happens in every sport. I always figured that if you bring something new to the sport, eventually people will embrace it.
John Lewis

If you are a 40-year-old lawyer or an architect, you can't train as crazy as a 20-year-old student. Also, you can't afford to get injured because you don't make a living with jiu-jitsu. Does it mean you can't get a black belt? No. Of course, you can!
Helio "Soneca" Moreira

Tournament competition teaches a judoka not so much how to fight but how to apply a variety of techniques in a safe environment so that he eventually transcends fear and develops self-confidence.
Jason Morris

I truly believe that by incorporating a physical discipline such as jiu-jitsu into our lives, we can balance and improve our overall existence.
Nino Schembri

Most are scared to train because they think they will get hurt. People need to realize that BJJ is the art of gentleness.
Marcio Feitosa

It is true that to go forward you have to leave things behind, but I'm happy because what judo represents today is something bigger that what it was in the past.
Mike Swain

Look for a good sensei, a good organization and work for them and with them. Don't forget; if you don't respect your sensei, how can you expect respect when you become one?
Jon Bluming

Hardcore weight training, running and stretching are not beneficial for a jiu-jitsu practitioner. The weight training, the running and the stretching exercises have to be adapted and fit into the jiu-jitsu format of moving the human body.

Leo Vieira

In the past, an instructor of mine would tell me to do something a certain way because the master who invented it had a fifth degree black belt. So what? If he never tried it in a real fight then I'm not interested in learning it.
Bas Rutten

Every practitioner needs to evaluate their training and know where they are going and what they really need to work on. There are many important elements that a practitioner has to develop before they get into a more complex technical approach.
Carlos "Caique" Elias

My advice to those who teach Brazilian jiu-jitsu, however, is that they should incorporate more classes for those people who are not athletes. There are many people out there who don't have the physical attributes of these athletes—people who are normal citizens, who go to work, have family lives and who would like to learn the art for fun and exercise.
Carlos Gracie Jr

America is an eclectic country by nature, it's a tapestry of many cultures and I guess that's the attitude that opens your eyes and doesn't make you feel guilty if you change something from the past in order to make it better.
Eric Paulson

My overall philosophy is very direct and simple; your game should be based on fitness and technique. Period.
Frank Shamrock

Grappling is great but there are situations when you just don't want to grapple.
Gokor Chivichyan

The fighters nowadays use a lot of strength and force when they fight. I never used those because I have always fought bigger and stronger opponents. It could have been suicidal to do it. My strategy was always based on technique, not strength.
Helio Gracie

Fear is not a good thing. Courage and confidence, balanced with realistic training and preparation, are what you want to increase.
Matt Furey

To a true jiu-jitsu practitioner the words "try" and "impossible" do not exist—you simply execute a technique when the situation warrants it.
Renato Magno

My personal training involves the physical part including the conditioning and jiu-jitsu techniques and the spiritual or mental.
Rickson Gracie

The motto at the Gracie Academy is there is no such a thing as a good or a bad student. All the students are the same. There is such a thing as a good or a bad teacher.
Rorion Gracie

Jiu-jitsu is an extremely important part of my life. It gave me direction when I was young, and it gave me the opportunity to meet great people who I have developed close ties and relationships with.
Wander Braga

I'm an athlete. I don't get caught up in all that talk. I train, step into the Octagon and fight. That's all there is for me. They can say what they want.
Randy Couture

New students should learn how to be patient and remember to always show respect for your partners.
Paulo Gillobel

To be able to fight, you need to stay within your style. I won't try to change it; I'll just make the right adjustments.
Royce Gracie

People are afraid of changes, but they're usually for the better. Intelligent people get used to change more quickly than others.
John Lewis

Train jiu-jitsu first, if it is jiu-jitsu you are interested in. Then, when you get some extra time, use it for additional training that allows you to improve the physical aspects necessary to excel in the art.
Helio "Soneca" Moreira

The best thing for judo is judo. Period. Beyond that, an athlete needs to find a coach who can create a training plan that allows him to reach the top.
Jason Morris

Never give up and train as hard as you can. This is a basic principle in all the budo arts.
Mike Swain

More exercising does not necessarily mean better results. You have to be specific in what you do and how you do it; otherwise, you risk wasting your time.
Leo Vieira

I'm very skeptical about claims that because a street fighter has 1000 wins, his technique must be good. So what? I can make a record of 50-0 in one night in a bar if I want. People on the street are not trained fighters, so that also is a dumb comment. You have to try a technique for yourself and see if it works for you.
Bas Rutten

If your main goal is just to protect yourself, then develop a very strong base with the fundamental techniques and don't go crazy trying to learn 1,000 different techniques. Stick to the basics because is out of the basic techniques that any new maneuver will come.
Carlos "Caique" Elias

Teachers should incorporate more classes into their academies where the training is more relaxed and more natural—where the emphasis relies on learning proper basic techniques and the physical demands are not like those for people who are going to compete.
Carlos Gracie Jr

As an instructor who cares for his students, I'm perplexed to see how other instructors are extremely concerned about giving their students freedom to go and train in other systems.
Eric Paulson

In martial arts in general, to maintain the vitality of our chosen art, you must put aside prejudices and inflexibility and be open to any innovation that would result in an improvement of what you are doing.
Frank Shamrock

The number one priority should be your cardiovascular conditioning. If you don't have good wind, it won't matter how good technically you are because you won't be able to execute your moves.
Gokor Chivichyan

Although it could be advantageous for our opponents, I believe that jiu-jitsu should be represented by a fighter wearing a gi.
Helio Gracie

Martial arts are a great tool if you know how to use the different mental and philosophical aspects for self-improvement. Enrolling in a martial arts school was the best thing I ever did.
Oleg Taktarov

In all martial arts, sincerity is essential to building a credible technique, although many people can't see the relationship between sincerity and the actual physical movements of jiu-jitsu.
Renato Magno

I know time changes a lot of things and sometimes not for the best. When my Japanese friends in Judo lost in 1970 in Paris the world title I was very sad, even if it was my countryman Anton Geesink who won, but that day it was the begin of an era. The Japanese hegemony was finally broken and nowadays anybody can win in world karate tournaments or Olympic judo.
Jon Bluming

Every day I wake up, thinking it's an excellent day to enjoy a day on the beach, an excellent day to fight, or an excellent day to die. So I'm always prepared for whatever happens.
Rickson Gracie

Properly performed, revealing knowledge to another is a deeply involving, almost symbiotic exercise.
Rorion Gracie

All my existence evolves around jiu-jitsu and only my family is more important to me.
Wander Braga

Train hard and train smart. Don't forget that every aspect of preparation is important and that includes the physical training, the diet and nutrition, the rest, the psychological.
Randy Couture

Try to focus on what you are doing with determination. Have the courage to train with everyone and to balance all the aspects of your life.
Paulo Gillobel

Being a Gracie doesn't just mean being a family member, it also means being a student and a member of the world jiu-jitsu community.
Royce Gracie

If someone wants to be a champion, he has to train like a champion. Whether you're talking about being a local gym champion, a city champion, a state or even world champion, you have to work hard.
John Lewis

Everything you do must have a purpose or an application to enhance your skills as a jiu-jitsu practitioner.
Helio "Soneca" Moreira

Supplementary training will, however, bring a new high level to judo practice. But, of course, it won't produce miracles overnight.
Jason Morris

Find a teacher that is an example to follow—not only in jiu-jitsu— but also as a human being. Have faith in everything you do, leave room to learn from others and always be humble.
Leo Vieira

If you train, do it 100 percent. Don't train, come home, and then not think about it anymore. Lock it up in your mind; go over it again and again. If you really want to learn how to fight, then think about fighting night and day.
Bas Rutten

Unfortunately, there are many practitioners these days who pay too much attention to the advanced techniques when they should be working on the basics.
Carlos "Caique" Elias

I would like to see more classes where the true essence of jiu-jitsu is being taught. This is what will allow jiu-jitsu to attract the general public. Otherwise, the sport will die out and fewer and fewer students will come to train.
Carlos Gracie Jr

After I retired from Shooto I had to find a different approach to what I was doing. It's bad when you go to train and your shoes are still wet from the previous workout or your gloves have no time to dry out. You train, you eat, you sleep and go back to train again. Suddenly you reach a point where is not fun to train anymore.
Eric Paulson

My body today does not want to do the things I used to do but once warmed up I can still kick serious butt. Believe me. But it is mostly the mind, which is working in high gear all the time.
Jon Bluming

I have a style that has no rules, that's one of the reasons why I don't really like the grappling events. I'm not a pretty good grappler or a wrestler, you know, but I am a very good submission fighter.
Frank Shamrock

Technical skill isn't enough. Accept the fact the weight and strength training has to be one of your priorities.
Gokor Chivichyan

What is an "old" technique? This is ridiculous! The problem lies in that modern practitioners are stronger than in the past—they don't really need to polish their technique to make a basic technique work because they compensate with brute force.
Helio Gracie

You need to be serious and perseverant in your training, otherwise your training will have no value.
Renato Magno

There are natural stages in the life of a martial artist but it takes effort to move from one to the next.
Hayward Nishioka

I have been always mentally prepared to fight so the spiritual aspect is not something that takes me a long time. I can get into that mood in a very short time.
Rickson Gracie

A sincere teacher, a devoted teacher, does not stand aloof and in judgment as his pupil struggles along his path.
Rorion Gracie

I am truly grateful to the Gracie family for developing this great art and for working hard to spread it around the world.
Wander Braga

Always be a gentleman, regardless if you win or lose. Don't forget that your opponent is the one who brings the best out of you.
Randy Couture

The UFC used to be style against style. Now it is fighter against fighter. It's man against man.
Royce Gracie

Keep in mind that this supplementary training should be specific or you'll be wasting your time.
Helio "Soneca" Moreira

Modern judo is blend of the most effective grappling techniques and principles into an organized and integrated structure that meet Olympic requirements.
Jason Morris

The practice of jiu-jitsu in our daily lives gives us energy and a fresh approach to things.
Nino Schembri

Fear tells you that you are in a tough situation so you need to be alert. When the adrenaline comes into your body, you can use it to make yourself stronger.
Marcio Feitosa

Everything is in constant change and the changes are in small increments. Often they are so small that people don't see the difference, and everybody thinks that judo is the same.
Hayward Nishioka

In martial arts, as in life, you are expected to mean what you say.
Shizuya Sato

Photographs

www.ingramcontent.com/pod-product-compliance
Lightning Source LLC
Chambersburg PA
CBHW072222270326
41930CB00010B/1955